The Naturalist Companio

A Field Guide to Observing
and Understanding Wildlife

Dave Hall

MOUNTAINEERS
BOOKS

MOUNTAINEERS BOOKS is dedicated to the exploration, preservation, and enjoyment of outdoor and wilderness areas.

1001 SW Klickitat Way, Suite 201, Seattle, WA 98134
800-553-4453, www.mountaineersbooks.org

Distributed in the United Kingdom by Cordee, www.cordee.co.uk
25 24 23 22   1 2 3 4 5

Copyeditor: Lorraine Anderson
Design and layout: Patrick Barber
All photographs by the author unless credited otherwise
Front cover photographs, top to bottom: *The red fox is a very adaptable species. These incredible hunters are found in a variety of habitats ranging from deep wilderness to urban areas.* (iStock/RT-Images); *The eastern bluebird has made a significant comeback in recent decades, largely due to the placement of specialized bird houses.* (iStock/SteveByland)
Back cover photographs, top to bottom: *Red-tailed hawks range and breed throughout a huge portion of North America. They can be found in northern Canada, the interior of Alaska and south into Panama.* (iStock/lavin photography); *Frogs of all sorts can be found throughout North America. These sensitive amphibians help indicate the relative health of ecosystems.*
Frontispiece: *Bobcat range over the vast majority of the US and southern Canada. Although common, bobcats are incredibly stealthy and can be challenging to spot.* (iStock/mtnmichelle)
Page 6: *Pika are small mammals related to rabbits that live in mountainous regions of western North America. Pika are preyed upon by a variety of predators such as fox, birds of prey, and weasels.* (iStock/Murphy_Skewchuk)

Library of Congress Cataloging-in-Publication data is on file for this title at https://lccn.loc.gov/2021057745.
The ebook record is on file at https://lccn.loc.gov/2021057746.

Mountaineers Books titles may be purchased for corporate, educational, or other promotional sales, and our authors are available for a wide range of events. For information on special discounts or booking an author, contact our customer service at 800-553-4453 or mbooks@mountaineersbooks.org.

Printed on FSC®-certified materials

ISBN (paperback): 978-1-68051-576-3
ISBN (ebook): 978-1-68051-577-0

An independent nonprofit publisher since 1960

To Jon, who was a kind person,
a good friend, and a caring father

Contents

Why Observe Wildlife?

Nature is a part of our humanity, and
without some awareness and experience of
that divine mystery man ceases to be man.

—HENRY BESTON, *THE OUTERMOST HOUSE*

One day I enter a mature woodland bordering an upscale neighborhood just outside the city of Ithaca, New York. Houses flank one side of this sloped habitat. The bottom edge is bound by a winding road that parallels a state highway. Despite the steady stream of traffic, I know that given even limited space and enough resources, wildlife can exist practically anywhere, and I'm here to see what I can find.

I park and exit my vehicle as quietly as possible. I have to be mindful from the outset: slamming doors and idling engines might put the forest's inhabitants on alert. I follow a deer trail up a steep slope from the road and into the forest. Each of my steps is restrained and purposeful. My eyes glance up and over the lip of the bank. I stop, scan, and wait.

When I reach the summit and enter the forest I continue to move cautiously, making no sound, toward a large downed white oak. I pause to soak in the warm fall day and peek behind the fallen timber—a favorite place for deer to bed. My efforts at stealth are rewarded when I discover a sleeping red fox. She's nestled into a warm bed of leaves where sunlight pours in through an opening in the canopy. The forest is calm.

As I sit and watch, several white-tailed deer come bounding through the thicket. I'm not sure what's caused them to alarm. They run past me at a distance of fifty yards, and the fox sits up and takes notice. The deer continue through the understory and settle down at the far edge of the woods before slipping out of sight. The movement of the awakened fox draws the attention of several species of bird, including black-capped chickadee, tufted titmouse, and white-breasted nuthatch. A gray squirrel and a nearby chipmunk have also become upset. Because of the chorus of alarms that follow, I'm able to keep track of her as she moves beyond my range of vision.

I continue to sit and wait as a second alarm rises about a hundred yards to the north. Songbirds are chattering from the treetops. It could be a red-tailed hawk. Moments later my suspicions are confirmed as a mature bird of prey slices through the forest and lands in the trees above where the fox was bedded. The hawk flies away soon after, and I catch a final glimpse of the fox as she trots off into the brush.

For as long as I can remember, I have been interested in watching animals. As a child, on long drives I would challenge myself by trying to spot the deer and hawks and whatever else made its home near the highway. My childhood friend Don Vizzi and I spent many afternoons quietly making our way through the local fields near the University of Buffalo in hopes of seeing a monster buck or calling in, or attracting, an elusive red fox. Don is one of my dearest and oldest friends from my youth. We met when I was around eleven and he was nine, when

---

Cottontail rabbits have excellent hearing and are masters of holding still until bolting at the last possible moment. (iStock/mirceaux)

his family moved in down the street from mine in Amherst, New York. We fished in tributaries that led to the Niagara, catching huge carp, sheepshead, and eventually, as the waters cleaned, big rainbows. He was my one friend during my formative years who had, and still has, this bug.

As we grew older, Don and the rest of our crew would venture farther from home to places like the Adirondacks as well as Algonquin Provincial Park in Ontario. Algonquin especially brought us up close to many of the inhabitants of the North Woods, including otter, loons, and a lot of moose. As we inflicted a sort of rite of passage upon ourselves, we grew closer as friends and subliminally learned what it might feel like to be something other than a product of the modern world. We learned how to move quietly, read the patterns of nature, and understand the life cycles of the wildlife around us. For me, the seeds of something ancient were planted during those journeys, and they have continued to grow to this day.

Now, having worked with individuals of all ages in the outdoors for almost thirty years as a naturalist, Adirondack guide, and primitive skills instructor, I continue to be inspired to pass these lessons along, sharing skills that once were part of our innate humanness. Whether you're a backyard naturalist, backpacker, seasoned field biologist, skilled hunter, or someone completely new to nature observation, these ancient techniques and perspectives will not only bring you a greater understanding of and closeness to wildlife but also change how you see your place on our planet.

For most of human history, understanding animals was part of an array of skills that helped us to survive and shaped our development. For our ancestral forebearers, observing animals and their behaviors was a vital necessity. Animals were considered powerful and wise teachers. Knowledge of each species' routines and vulnerabilities—coupled with the ability to infiltrate the landscape—enabled cultures to not only exist but also thrive and stay safe.

But now, this type of knowledge, once common, is dwindling to the point of extinction. "Nature-deficit disorder," a term coined by naturalist Richard Louv, describes how we suffer when we spend too little time in wilderness settings. In *Last Child in the Woods*, Louv reflects on the nurturing and invigorating influence that connecting with nature has on our lives. The US Forest Service's "Discover the Forest" campaign responds to our loss of connection by seeking to inspire families to explore local parks and forests. I believe we can all benefit from, and augment our lives through, a deeper understanding of our environment. Furthermore, I believe animals have much to teach us about our innate humanness. In our not-so-distant past, part of what it meant to be human was a deep and abiding understanding of and respect for animal wisdom.

Where Can You Go to Spot Wildlife?

The quick answer is: anywhere. National parks and other wilderness areas are wonderful—yet often distant—treasures, but in actuality the drama and excitement of discovering wildlife are available close to home, no matter where you live. Some of my favorite and most fruitful places to go include the following:

- city parks
- the edges of golf courses
- local preserves, including land trust properties, state forests, and wild spaces held by our local institutions such as universities
- local waterways, including small creeks, rivers, wetlands, and ponds
- railway corridors
- green areas within on-ramps to highways
- easily overlooked places such as the small woods behind the local big box store, the untended thicket at the edge of a parking lot, or the pile of tires behind the mechanic's shop that has offered shelter to an urban woodchuck

This list could go on and on. Be open to recognizing that birds, insects, reptiles, larger animals, and aquatic-based life-forms are everywhere.

Two pervasive (and opposing) views seem to exist regarding our relationship with the natural world. One is that humans are separate from nature. In this paradigm we are visitors, alien sightseers venturing into uncharted realms. The other is that humans are a part of nature. Here we are full participants, ultimately acting as stewards of the land.

It is my intention to help bring you toward the second, and formerly common, understanding of your relationship with the world by imparting traditional knowledge and skills I've acquired over my lifetime. My aim is to share how to see without being seen, to move

The biological impulse to spawn has led these sockeye salmon from the deep waters of the Pacific into a shallow tributary. Understanding cycles such as this one can assist you in finding wildlife you hope to see. (iStock/birdimages)

without being heard, to interpret the calls and behavior of our animal kin, and occasionally to employ this knowledge to influence an animal's behavior.

Through the judicious use of historic hunting and stealth techniques, I've gained consistent access to nature's most hidden secrets. I have called in foxes by mimicking wounded prey. I have learned to become invisible to spawning fish so I can catch them with my bare hands. And I have interpreted the alarm cries of crows to locate great horned owls. Simply put, observing wildlife is one of my greatest joys, and becoming a more learned and patient observer has aided me in becoming a more proficient naturalist. I'll never forget the excitement of seeing a litter of wild dogs frolicking outside their den or watching a great blue heron stalk along the shores of a wetland.

With this book, I hope to both enrich and strengthen your bond with the outdoors by providing practical and ethical tools that will improve the quality and depth of your outdoor experiences.

This book is organized to build from the critical fundamentals to more advanced perspectives and skills. Successive chapters explore the importance of camouflage, use of the senses, understanding animal language and behavior, how to capitalize on a familiarity with annual cycles, the art of tracking and recognizing signs, and calling. I address ways you can propagate a love for the outdoors through what I've dubbed backyard awareness. In addition, you will learn to get the most out of limited time spent in the field by learning to recognize wildlife hot spots and the best times of day and seasons to visit these places. Finally, I speak to the phenomenon I call spontaneous acceptance, where under the right circumstances, humans can be accepted by their wild kin as a benign and perhaps benevolent part of the landscape.

Each chapter begins with a personal story or anecdote to help demonstrate and frame the content to be shared. I then move into the hard skills and critical perspectives. After the first chapter, each chapter concludes with suggested exercises that are designed to help build good habits.

The skills detailed in these pages are experimental (and experiential) in nature. Cast aside any preconceptions you might have; even for the most seasoned naturalist, there's always something new to learn. It isn't always easy to know what is happening in regard to animal behavior and interactions, and I regularly find myself unsure about what it is I am witnessing. This is to be expected, as we can't possibly know everything. Explanations can sometimes take a long while to reveal themselves, and some things may remain a mystery for a lifetime.

It's important to remember that no guidebook can take the place of time spent in the field. Though I believe the information in this book is invaluable, no one can learn the subtleties of nature awareness from reading alone. Give yourself the gift of time outdoors and do your best to let go of agenda and expectation. The skills presented here can be the keys to unlocking a part of yourself that has been buried deep. This awakening of new perceptions should be exciting, joyous, and fun, changing how you feel about the world around you in a substantial and positive way.

CHAPTER 1

Preparing to Observe Wildlife

Wilderness is not only a haven for native plants and animals but it is also a refuge from society. It's a place to go to hear the wind and little else, see the stars and the galaxies, smell the pine trees, feel the cold water, touch the sky and the ground at the same time, listen to coyotes, eat the fresh snow, walk across the desert sands, and realize why it's good to go outside of the city and the suburbs. Fortunately, there is wilderness just outside the limits of the cities and the suburbs in most of the United States, especially in the West.

—JOHN MUIR

Early in the summer of 1988, when I was twenty years old, my father and I set out on a road trip that took us to Mount Rushmore and Devils Tower and across the Badlands. Midway through our journey we stopped in South Dakota's Custer State Park.

Custer is famous for its herds of wild bison; we were eager to catch a glimpse of these enduring symbols of America's frontier.

After checking into a nearby lodge, my father and I walked toward the park's visitor center. Several female bison passed in front of us as we made our way down a dirt road, but they showed little interest in our presence and we continued on. Nearer the center we spotted two male bison foraging in the adjoining meadow. We split up. My father walked a tree-lined drive that led to the building's entrance as I took the somewhat shorter route through the meadow. I wasn't concerned. The bison were grazing more than a hundred yards away.

When I was about halfway across the meadow, one of the bison suddenly charged. I remember initially feeling amused as I broke into a lazy jog. But my amusement quickly turned to terror when I realized I was about to be overtaken. With no trees to climb and no boulders for refuge, I did the only thing I could—I fell to the ground and played dead. The bison slowed to a gallop and then a trot, finally coming to rest fifty feet away.

As I lay curled up in the meadow, the other bison began aggressively pawing the earth. I could feel the ground shake. I was scared but I remained still, eyeing the pair from beneath my curled arms. Then the second bison charged, closing the gap to fifteen feet in a matter of seconds.

I thought that was it. I expected to die. But I was lucky. For some reason, at the last instant, the bison veered away, stopped, and resumed grazing. Unable to move, I continued to lie in the grass. Someone at the visitor center observed my predicament and drove his truck into the meadow, parking the vehicle between the two bison and me. Trembling, I stood up and leapt into the cab. The man drove me back to the center to rendezvous with my father, who had stood by, watching helplessly as the scene unfolded.

PREVIOUS IMAGE Bison are large and powerful herbivores that demand respect. It was with large males such as these that I had my close encounter—a hard lesson that almost cost me my life. Ever since that event I have been much more careful and respectful when I am around large and potentially dangerous animals. (Melissa Groo)

What lessons can we learn from this event? They involve understanding safety, responsibility, and ethics in all wildlife encounters. I would be remiss not to discuss these three crucial topics right at the beginning.

Safety

It is my greatest hope that this book will lead you outside, equipped with new perspectives and tools. The skills you will learn here can allow for incredibly close access to wildlife. Use these skills wisely and always err on the side of caution. The record shows that the most significant threat to our safety in the great outdoors is ourselves. *At no time should you knowingly approach animals that have the ability to harm you.*

At Custer State Park, I was young and uninformed and ultimately made a bad choice. This kind of mistake happens most often in areas where the lines separating the human-oriented and natural worlds become blurred—most notably in places like our national and state parks. Injuries and rare fatalities have occurred in places like Yellowstone and Custer State Park as the result of tourists' belief that because animals live in a park, they are somehow more docile. Nothing could be further from the truth. Although statistically rare, dangerous encounters with wildlife can and do happen, both in parks and beyond.

It should go without saying that there are many hazards in the world, and the uninformed or flippant person can easily get in an undesirable situation in the great outdoors. Nature is full of plants that can cut or sting you, or even kill you if ingested. Gravity is the undoing of many people in the context of outdoor adventure. But with education, most of the dangers can be eliminated or at least mitigated. Where I live, in central New York State, I have learned which plants are poisonous and which are edible and utilitarian. I also keep an eye on the weather and stay aware of seasonal hazards. We have many waterfalls and gorges that require respect. Our waterways, generally inviting places to cool off during the summer, can quickly become flooded and dangerous after a heavy rain. During the summer we have a regular threat of thunderstorms and have had

Until you are a seasoned naturalist, it is best to avoid tasting plants that are unknown. Where I live, there are plants such as poisonous water hemlock that can kill a person. By the same token, to ensure you don't pick up a venomous snake, be sure to properly identify it first. Understanding the dangers doesn't mean you should be paranoid about going outside; rather, it gives you another avenue to pursue in your learning about the natural world. Knowing how to identify plants and other possible hazards can give you greater confidence. An excellent book I have referred to many times over the years is *A Field Guide to Venomous Animals and Poisonous Plants*, by Steven Foster and Roger Caras, in the Peterson Field Guide Series.

an increasing number of tornado threats. In colder months I dress to protect myself from wet, windy, and snowy conditions. If I venture into the mountains, I know this region can be unforgiving and demands great consideration and preparation, especially if I choose to explore these areas in winter.

One way to help alleviate fear and gain confidence is simply to learn what hazards are found in your area or any place you are planning to travel to. And within the context of the place, understand what the consequences might be if you encounter any of those hazards. For example, on a fifteen-day canoe trip in Ontario in 2018, I became ever more vigilant about my choices, knowing that something as simple as a sprained ankle could leave me stuck for days, unable to carry my boat over the next portage trail. Learning to recognize hazards and how to

RIGHT Raccoons are highly adaptable animals that live in a variety of settings, and the densest numbers of them can often be found in urban areas. Raccoons are opportunistic and omnivorous, known to eat fruits, eggs, nuts, crayfish, and frogs. They will also take advantage of human food sources, like unprotected pet food, gardens, and garbage containers. (iStock/JMichl)

Guidelines for Thoughtful Engagement

○ **Avoid causing unnecessary disturbance or stress to wildlife.**

○ **Be considerate of rare species, species of concern, and species that live in sensitive habitats.** It is up to you to learn the species in your region. If you are unsure of an animal's status, be sure to identify it before any attempt to influence it.

○ **Remain sensitive to seasonal pressures.** Certain times of the year and situations can be especially trying for animals. (Chapters 4 and 5 go into more detail about animal behaviors and vulnerabilities.)

○ **Be extra considerate around animals that are raising young.**

○ **Influencing animals to come closer is often a possibility and should be done in responsible ways.** Be cognizant of the time of year if you choose to call. Winter birds, for example, may have a limited food supply and may be operating with a very small energy reserve.

○ **Show respect for private and public property, as well as consideration for other people.**

○ **If you use the skills in this book to hunt, refrain from participating in wildlife killing contests.** Follow local laws and do your best to fully utilize the animal you have taken. Two excellent books on this topic are *Deerskins into Buckskins* by Matt Richards and *Primitive Technology II: Ancestral Skills*, edited by David Wescott.

avoid or deal with them is all part of the path to becoming a skilled naturalist.

Responsibility

It is your responsibility to know when and where you can go off trail. The myriad of land agencies across our country have a variety of different regulations. Throughout the US, there are many national parks,

- **Limit baiting, if legal, so as not to habituate animals in an adverse way.**

My friend and accomplished wildlife photographer Melissa Groo always follows specific guidelines to ensure the welfare of her intended quarry. According to "Audubon's Guide to Ethical Bird Photography and Videography," which she helped craft, "The first essential element in bird photography is a sincere respect for the birds and their environment. In any conflict of interest, the well-being of the birds and their habitats must come before the ambitions of the photographer." (You can find the full list of guidelines on the Audubon website at audubon.org.) Melissa's adherence to these parameters has yielded remarkable success. She has photographed bobcats, foxes, lions, puffins, birds of prey, grizzlies, and elephants—all in their natural habitats. And as her work illustrates, ethics and achievement are not mutually exclusive.

When Melissa photographs piping plovers, for example, she approaches the shorebirds at an indirect angle and from a great distance and then settles in and observes for a while. She may eventually move a bit closer but not directly toward the birds, often anticipating their direction of travel. Very often, on their own, the plovers move closer, so close that she is surrounded by them.

wilderness areas, national forests, state forests, land trust preserves, and various urban, county, and state parks. Each place has its own rules regarding where you can go and what you can do. In most preserves, for instance, visitors are asked to stay on the trail or boardwalk. On the other end of the spectrum, you often are free to wander in less sensitive state forests. Always be mindful of fragile and rare ecosystems, taking care to avoid disturbing rare plants and inhabitants wherever you are.

It is also up to you to learn if collecting discoveries such as skulls or antlers is allowed where you are visiting. The National Park Service, for example, is bound by Title 36 of the Code of Federal Regulations to prohibit the removal of any natural, cultural, and archeological resources, which include antlers, bones, skulls, nests, rocks, flowers, and artifacts like arrowheads, potsherds, or old bottles and cans. Most government agencies, private reserves, or nonprofit conservation groups that regulate wild places ask visitors to not take anything from their properties. On the other hand, I have many skulls, bones, and sets of antlers I have collected legally for teaching purposes, either from my own forest or from places that allow collection.

Ethics

I encourage you to observe, listen, and occasionally influence animal behavior in a way that ethically serves your goals. There's nothing unethical about killing an animal if your survival calls for it or if you're following legal guidelines regarding what you can take and in what seasons and hunt in an ethical manner. But selfish utilization when the greater well-being of wildlife isn't considered, such as teasing or unnecessarily stressing an animal, is another matter. Under no circumstances do I endorse using the skills this book teaches for the unethical exploitation of wildlife and the planet.

Some readers may find that a few of the skills presented in this book go against the grain of what they have been taught or hold in their minds as the right thing to do. For example, influencing or calling an animal could be seen as unnecessarily stressing wildlife. But to my way of thinking, we should only attempt to responsibly influence an animal after considerable study and a deep immersion in the lives of such animals around us. Thus, influencing and calling are based on a foundation of appreciation and understanding.

Another example of possible concern is the idea of intercepting a bird or animal through knowledge of its most vulnerable times of year. This kind of intimate knowledge of an animal's lifeways was exactly what our ancestors relied upon to help ensure food for the winter. In her acclaimed book *Indian Fishing*, Hilary Stewart records in remarkable

The red eft is the terrestrial stage of the red spotted newt. These plentiful amphibians are commonly seen in damp woodlands. (iStock/Douglas Rissing)

line drawings and text the multitude of ways the Indigenous people of the Northwest and coastal Canada used traps, weirs, spears, and nets based on their knowledge of seasonal patterns to ensure full larders. These methods were sustainable and respected the gifts that the sea offered by taking only what was needed. It wasn't until the European era that the great runs of salmon became compromised. Today, knowledge of the seasonal vulnerabilities of wildlife comes with great responsibility. It should not be used outside of the context of learning, legal hunting, or gaining information that can help with conservation and scientific understanding.

We are in the midst of a period of extinction, and it's good to remember that humans are the cause of this great loss. We have been inflicting our agenda of dominance on the planet for a relatively short time, but the consequences have been catastrophic. Now we face a choice between forging ahead with our destructive ways of thinking—our fixation on the GNP, our quest to constantly produce more and conquer more—or learning from the past and returning to the lifeway skills of people who lived, until recently, alongside animals in relative harmony. Perhaps on that alternative path we might learn something ancient that is inherently part of who we are.

Each and every one of us is hardwired to be tied to the earth. It should be alarming that I need to point this out and that we need to push ourselves and our children to get outdoors and spend time in nature. I often wonder if the goals of the modern world conspire against not only the planet but also our psychological and spiritual needs. There is an eroding force at play. It is time to stop, and to create a relationship with animals based on respect, reverence, and honor.

Reverence for animals can take many forms. Many of the skills and much of the knowledge found in these pages have roots in hunting, the kind done by hunters who feel great reverence for the animals they kill. That might be hard for many people to hear, but be careful not to judge. To me the act of hunting has always been a deliberate act of ritual and respect that has connected me in a significant way to the forest and the deer that live within it. These skills can serve modern photographers, birders, and field biologists just as well.

It is also important to note that beyond our species' ability to affect wildlife negatively on a grand scale, our personal choices have consequences for the wildlife in our immediate surroundings as well. We hit animals with our cars, till under animal homes as we farm, and poison waterways with our runoff. Even our more innocent actions regularly affect animals. Sit quietly in any natural area near a bike or hiking trail, and it doesn't take long to notice that animals adapt how they go about their business to a disproportionate degree based on human presence. Most people are oblivious to these kinds of effects.

There can be a wide gap between what is legal and what is moral. For example, we can fly in airplanes, yet their carbon emissions alone have arguably caused significant harm to the planet. So while of course it is legal to use airplanes, there is an argument to be made about the morality of doing so. If, on the other hand, I catch a white sucker using just my hands, an ancient practice that requires patience and knowledge and one I consider to be moral, I could get a ticket if I'm in New York State because this way of catching fish is not legal there.

I feel strongly that animals should be treated with respect and consideration (even if that means we sometimes eat and utilize them). Some of my "Guidelines for Thoughtful Engagement" may seem paradoxical in that I suggest you be considerate while teaching skills you could use to put food on your table. The duty of using the skills responsibly rests with you.

Preparing for Survival and Your Body's Needs

It is important to note that your number one goal is to come home safely at the end of your intended outing. Being prepared with proper gear and clothing and having strong navigation and survival skills is essential. It is one thing to go into a modest-sized county park with minimal knowledge or gear but quite another to venture into a big wilderness area without being properly prepared and informed about potential hazards. If you're going into the backcountry, you should travel with someone who is experienced or take a course that covers at least orienteering and basic first aid and survival. Other skills such as aidless navigation and self-rescue can also be helpful for the serious wilderness adventurer.

Most people get into trouble in natural areas out of ignorance. The woods that once seemed bright and welcoming can quickly turn ominous if you get lost; panic sets in, and you realize you don't have what you need to find your way out, alert rescue, or meet your immediate survival demands.

A quick and unscientific way to organize your understanding around survival is the rule of threes. This memory device is designed to help you understand your body's priorities so you can prepare properly for outings and stay focused on the most important elements of survival should you find yourself in a critical situation.

The Rule of Threes
Don't go for more than:

- **Three minutes without oxygen.** In a situation where someone has stopped breathing for any reason, as in drowning, using CPR is the most critical step. Know this skill before venturing into the backcountry.
- **Three hours in an extreme environment (either hot or cold).** This means avoiding hypothermia, which is a dangerous drop in body temperature, as well as heat exhaustion and heat stroke. Your goal should be to keep your body temperature where nature meant it to be, somewhere around 98.6 degrees, by being prepared with appropriate clothing and shelter.
- **Three days without water.** Having, or being able to procure, clean water is essential. The recommendation is to drink half your body weight in ounces of water each day, so plan accordingly when you go out.
- **Three weeks without food.** Going without food for a day or two is fine. Most of us have more than a bit of reserve on our bones, so the compulsion that many people feel in the initial hours of a survival situation to look for food should be recognized as actually being a lower priority. Energy should instead be spent on efforts to stay warm and hydrated.

I always go out with the intention of being able to meet my needs even in the worst possible situation I might reasonably encounter. What you bring with you may very much reflect your skill and comfort level with the outdoors and wilderness survival. I, for instance, always carry my cell phone, a quality lighter, and a good pocket knife. This is my bare minimum. The phone is there in case I become immobile because of a twisted ankle or something similar. The lighter helps me produce fire in the event of cold, and the knife helps me do everything else, such as build a new society from scratch.

If you have less survival knowledge, it is wise to travel with a bit more equipment to help meet your immediate needs. Where you are headed, the time of year, and your experience level all need to be taken into consideration. The list of basic "what if" items to keep in your pockets or pack is commonly known as the Ten Essentials.

The Ten Essentials

The point of the Ten Essentials, originated by The Mountaineers, has always been to answer two basic questions: Can you prevent emergencies and respond positively should one occur? And can you safely spend a night—or more—outside? So whether you're planning a short outing or simple day hike or a longer outdoor adventure, you should always carry at least the basic versions of these items with you. Use this list as a guide and tailor it to the needs of your outing.

1. **Navigation:** The five fundamentals are a map, altimeter, compass, GPS device, and a personal locator beacon or other device to contact emergency first responders.
2. **Headlamp:** Include spare batteries.
3. **Sun protection:** Wear sunglasses, sun-protective clothes, and broad-spectrum sunscreen rated at least SPF 30.
4. **First aid:** Basics include bandages; skin closures; gauze pads and dressings; roller bandage or wrap; tape; antiseptic; blister prevention and treatment supplies; nitrile gloves; tweezers; needle; nonprescription painkillers; anti-inflammatory, anti-diarrheal, and antihistamine tablets; topical antibiotic; and any important personal prescriptions, including an EpiPen if you are allergic to bee or hornet venom.
5. **Knife:** Also consider a multitool, strong tape, some cordage, and gear repair supplies.
6. **Fire:** Carry at least one butane lighter (or waterproof matches) and firestarter, such as chemical heat tabs, cotton balls soaked in petroleum jelly, or commercially prepared firestarter.

7. **Shelter:** In addition to a rain shell, carry a single-use bivy sack, plastic tube tent, or jumbo plastic trash bag.
8. **Extra food:** For shorter trips a one-day supply is reasonable.
9. **Extra water:** Carry sufficient water and have the skills and tools required to obtain and purify additional water
10. **Extra clothes:** Pack additional layers needed to survive the night in the worst conditions that your party may realistically encounter.

Beyond the Ten Essentials, you might also want to carry these items, depending on your destination and the season:

- reflective blanket
- cell phone
- whistle
- orange flagging
- paracord
- trekking poles to help with slippery, steep, or snowy conditions
- snowshoes for deeper snow

How to Dress

Carefully consider what to wear when seeking wildlife. Clothing can help keep you not only quiet and concealed but also warm and protected from the elements. Your destination, the season, and any potential weather you may encounter should all be considered when assembling your wardrobe. Choose items that are muted colors found in nature. Plaids and camouflage patterns can help break up your outline, but note that the most expensive outdoor clothing with the latest camouflage pattern will do you absolutely no good in seeing and getting close to wildlife if you are loud and moving around. I do not wear anything special, yet on a regular basis I find myself in close proximity to wildlife, going undetected because I am still and quiet.

As temperatures decrease, layering—simply wearing multiple lighter layers as opposed to one heavy one—gives you the option of taking off clothing so you don't overheat and start to sweat, or adding clothing to increase insulation so you don't start to shiver.

This resting deer is not only conserving energy but is also staying alert to potential threats as it lies still in the snow. (iStock/Michael-Tatman)

Cotton. Nondenim cotton is fine to wear in warm and hot weather. (Denim can be loud and constricting.) T-shirts and shorts made of cotton are light and cool, and when they get damp they draw heat away from the body. This quality that is so nice during the summer heat and in arid environments makes cotton a fabric that should be avoided at all costs when there is any chance of cool or colder temperatures. Many times over the years I have heard the reminder "cotton kills." Its quality of drawing heat away from the body when damp can cause hypothermia and make a situation worse. Garments made from synthetic or wool materials are better choices for cold or questionable weather.

Synthetics. Synthetic materials are some form of plastic. The downside is that synthetics are not sustainable. The upside is that they are found in all kinds of colors and camouflage patterns, and materials like synthetic fleece can be very quiet. Synthetics dry quickly and help keep you warm even when damp. Some synthetics, though, can hold onto odors, which is important to consider if you are trying to remain invisible to wildlife.

Wool. Wool is awesome. It is warm even when damp, lasts forever, and comes in great outdoorsy dull and camouflage patterns. Wool is a bit heavy, but I personally like the feel of a good weighty wool coat.

Down. There is nothing like down to help keep you warm. Down, though, has to be kept dry or it will lose its insulating ability. Down jackets can also be a bit noisy since the feathers are generally stuffed inside a nylon shell.

Waterproof layers. Outer layers that are waterproof are important, especially if you are heading deep into a natural area when rain or colder weather is in the forecast. Generally speaking, waterproof outer layers are a bit noisy, something for the observant naturalist wearing them to be aware of.

Wild clothing. Garments made from a tanned animal hide are what our forebearers wore. They are natural colored and smell natural.

It is also important to think about what goes on your feet. In warmer weather, when keeping your feet warm isn't an issue, try to wear thin-soled shoes or sandals that let your feet feel the ground. Wearing moccasins or going barefoot are also excellent options. As the weather gets colder, it is important to keep your feet insulated and well protected. Insulated mukluks that you make or purchase are ideal if you're interested in wearing soft and quiet footwear in the colder months.

Cold hands should be avoided by wearing quality insulated gloves, or better yet, mittens. When temperatures drop, I keep the idea of layering in mind and wear insulated leather mittens over insulated leather gloves.

Naturalist Gear

To aid you in observing wildlife and expanding your understanding, consider these items:

- journal with a pen or pencil
- binoculars

- camera
- field guides
- cell phone

I am not opposed to judicious use of technology when it comes to connecting with nature. There is nothing wrong with using binoculars or bringing a camera along to help you see or record what you have discovered. But smart phones, which you should have for safety, warrant special concern. I have seen so many people turn to their phone impulsively and let it become a distraction from being in the present moment. If you are going to bring your phone with you, make a promise to yourself that you will use it only for certain intended purposes or not at all.

Many apps available today may (or may not, depending on the person using them) help people connect with nature. One app I am familiar with lets the user take a photograph of a flower or bird and then offers suggestions as to what the species might be. When you are using this kind of resource, you can easily be lulled into a false sense of knowing with the click of a button. In comparison, when using a field guide to identify something, you generally have to look closely and pay attention to colors, markings, size, shape, habitat, and other variables. This kind of identification asks us to engage to a much greater degree than an app does.

I use apps as a way to confirm what I am seeing. Ultimately I think they are best used with a good field guide. The real test will come with time. Ask yourself: Are your skills being developed by using an app, or are they staying the same? The hope is that you will eventually be able to recognize a given animal or bird without an app.

CHAPTER 2

Invisibility and Movement

You learn that if you sit down in the woods
and wait, something happens.

—HENRY DAVID THOREAU

After a slow and careful approach across a wetland boardwalk at a local land trust reserve in Dryden, New York, I continue down a path toward a small animal trail that leads to a
beaver lodge tucked into a bank. The sun is about to set. I am slow
and cautious, knowing any false move could announce my presence.
As I get closer to the bank, I lower myself to crawl, taking extra care
to not make any noise. My efforts are rewarded. As I peer over the lip
of the slope, I find myself within ten feet of a young beaver working a
small willow branch. I lie on my belly, grateful for the experience. As I
watch, the adolescent goes about its work, and I hear a subtle rustling
behind me that I assume to be a chipmunk or bird. I can't risk being
noticed by turning around. An adult beaver, likely a parent, emerges
below and joins the young one. They speak to each other with endear-
ing high-pitched whines. To me these sounds seem to express love

and concern. Every so often I continue to hear a leaf rustle or a subtle movement in the brush. Again I assume it is a small creature. After a few minutes I cautiously slip back from the edge of the wetland and look behind me.

I am surprised to see four humans making their way, in the same careful manner as I did, toward the lodge. I quietly move past them and silently signal that there are animals below. I wait on the boardwalk, curious to find out how they learned to move with such deliberateness. I later learn the family of four—parents and two children—were practicing skills the kids learned at Primitive Pursuits, a program I founded in 1999 that focuses on ancestral living skills and nature awareness. I was happy to see these lessons put into practice. They knew the best time to visit the wetland (just before the sun went down), where to go, and how to move in the landscape to be rewarded with a wondrous experience.

The next week I find myself at the same wetland, sitting on a bench where the boardwalk ends. Four beavers are out and about, and the bench offers a perfect view. As I sit, I hear a car pull into the gravel parking lot about two hundred yards away. Despite how far away I am, I can hear music from the visitor's headphones as he emerges from his car. The man slams his door and heads down the trail toward the boardwalk on a power walk. The beavers sense something is out of baseline (more on this later) as the man quickly bounds over the bridge and heads their way. They freeze and listen, attempting to make sense of this impending threat. As the sound of the hiker's feet grows louder, the beavers disperse. One slips over the side of the dam. Another, closer to the main pool, slaps its tail in the water before submerging to the safety of the lodge. The other two simply vanish. As the man passes me, music blares from his headphones. This hiker has no idea how his energy has repelled the local residents.

PREVIOUS IMAGE To feed themselves, great blue herons must move with great intent to get within striking distance of their prey. These magnificent birds are known to eat fish and frogs along with mice, insects, and other field inhabitants. (iStock/Robert Winkler)

Over the years, experiences such as my encounter with the adolescent beaver and its parent have become more common for me. By employing fundamental skills of my ancestors, I've endeavored to do what's been done since time immemorial: connect with my environment in pragmatic and enriching ways. This is something other people who live close to the land have known how to do for millennia. The foundation of everything I will teach here is the skill of remaining invisible. Through invisibility one is able to observe, learn from, and question the actions and motivations of wildlife.

Before industrialization, humans relied on an intimate understanding of their environment to meet their needs. They interpreted tracks and signs to determine the intricacies of each animal's routines and vulnerabilities. They used cover and camouflage to their advantage. They listened, careful not to disturb smaller mammals and birds that might broadcast their arrival. Today, anyone can make use of these skills to become a more natural participant in the events that take place outdoors.

The intent of this chapter is to give you an understanding of the importance of invisibility and the tools to become invisible so you can be granted a front-row seat for the never-ending drama that continually unfolds around us. It is of the utmost importance to always consider the impact you're having on your surroundings and its inhabitants. Otherwise, you simply won't be in a position to court valuable encounters with wildlife. Ideally, the ethical and skilled observer keeps any clues about his or her presence to a minimum. This, combined with a vigorous curiosity, will give you access to worlds previously inaccessible.

The Concept of Baseline

Before we get into the fundamentals of invisibility, you must first grasp the concept of baseline. Baseline refers to behaviors or activities that support life. Generally speaking, baseline behaviors happen when an animal feels safe. Activities such as caring for young, grooming, and seeking out a mate tend to occur when an animal isn't worried about its safety. Baseline movements are usually energy efficient.

A crow heckles a hawk in an attempt to drive it out of its territory. When witnessing animal behavior such as this, a fundamental and very important question to ask yourself is "Am I seeing a baseline (life-supporting) or an alarming (life-protecting) behavior?"

A break in baseline indicates at the very least some sort of concern and at the very most a fear response to a deadly threat. Breaks in baseline are marked by heightened awareness, evasive tactics, alarms, and the struggle to avoid becoming a meal. Baseline is a relative thing. An animal such as a deer will likely show little concern if a fox happens by, but anything that can be hunted and eaten by a fox will surely have good reason to be concerned and show alarm. Baseline also points toward the law of energy conservation. (More on this in Chapter 4.) Because they are energy intensive, sprinting and running can be risky business.

Very often humans can be and are the source of a break in baseline for wildlife. It is critical for naturalists to become aware of how they are affecting baseline, with the goal of having their presence in the wild be accepted or, ideally, not noticed at all. The goal of invisibility is to avoid thoughtlessly breaking baseline and to remain unnoticed. Deliberate breaks in baseline in order to influence wildlife (discussed in Chapter 7) are employed only after a naturalist has a deep understanding of animal language and needs and can use this information in a purposeful way.

One of the resident garter snakes in my backyard successfully captures a toad. Both garter snakes and toads fill the dual role of predator and prey, depending on the situation.

Baseline is not the same everywhere for every animal. For example, wildlife in national parks often become quite accustomed to humans and see them as a nonthreat. When these same animals are found in places where they can be hunted, however, they remain vigilant. Baseline for predatory species varies, as those at the apex of the food chain are often the *cause* of an alarm or a disturbance in baseline. It is also important to note that even when a predator is afoot, there may be no alarm. Just as you and I can infiltrate the matrix of the wild, so too can predators such as canines, felines, and birds of prey enter an area unnoticed. But once a threat has been identified, the baseline is disrupted and the intensity of an alarm will often mirror the severity of that threat.

Remember that many animals fill the dual role of predator *and* prey. Because of this, baseline can sometimes be difficult to identify. The frogs that live in my pond are an excellent example of this. Frogs are amazing catchers of insects of all sorts but are also a food source for many potential predators.

The concept of baseline can also be applied to environments in general. A creek or river, for example, has a natural flow or rhythm to it. By carefully watching for breaks in normalcy, the attuned outdoorsperson can find clues to an animal's presence. Often it is an odd ripple or concentric rings that draw my attention to a muskrat, beaver, or spawning fish.

Baseline can change, depending on seasons and circumstances. As you learn to recognize the cyclical behaviors of animals (such as deer mating), you'll be able to anticipate and observe these behaviors. It is also important to note that baseline behaviors don't necessarily correlate with calm. At times some baseline behaviors can be very dramatic. Males fighting over territory, for example, can be very dramatic, but in general this behavior takes place only when they feel safe from predation.

Best Places and Times to Find Wildlife

Where should you sit (or for that matter, where should you sneak) so that you have the best chance of seeing the most wildlife? Begin by reviewing what animals need to survive: food, cover, shelter, water, and a territory to ensure life's other needs. Though these factors will differ depending on your subject, if you can find an area where all of these resources collide, you'll have discovered a good place to focus your energy.

A transition zone, edge area, or ecotone—all terms for where one habitat meets another—is a likely place to find wildlife. An example is where a forest meets a field. Such places enable animals to access myriad resources without expending a wealth of energy. These areas are generally excellent locations to identify prey species (or their sign). Where you find prey, you can generally expect predators. Once again, all things are relative to the situation and size of the wildlife you might find. For example, a miniature waterfall no more than a few inches

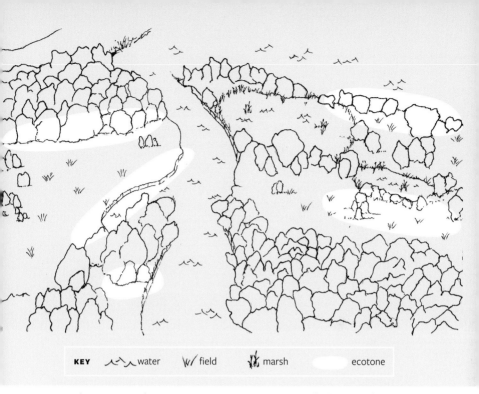

Many places serve as edge or transition zones or ecotones and offer local wildlife a multitude of options for food, shelter, and water.

high may not hold a large fish midsummer, but it might be an excellent place to look for water snakes in search of minnows.

What about time of day? In general, animals are most active when the sun is low on the horizon, either at dawn or dusk. This isn't to suggest you shouldn't test your skills at other times; it means only that you're more likely to have success during these periods. Don't be scared of the dark, either! Many animals are nocturnal and at their most active once the sun has set.

Weather can also impact an animal's activity level. In the Northeast, this phenomenon is best observed during early spring rains, when *Ambystoma maculatum*, the spotted salamander, begins its annual migratory journey. Returning to the same vernal pool year after year, these amphibians travel great distances in answer to their instinctual mating drive. It is not uncommon, in fact, to see a multitude of spotted

Bird and Animal Field Guides

There are many excellent field guides to help you identify wildlife. Many well-known guidebook series, like Audubon, offer regional guides, but here are some general guides I keep on my shelf:

- *Mammals of North America* by Roland W. Kays and Don E. Wilson
- *National Geographic Field Guide to the Birds of North America* by Jonathan Alderfer and Jon L. Dunn
- *Peterson Field Guide to Birds of North America* by Roger Tory Peterson
- *The Sibley Guide to Birds*, 2nd edition, by David Allen Sibley

salamanders crossing the road in late March or early April, leaving them susceptible to predation—or worse, passing vehicles.

Oncoming storms often lead to a spike in activity as animals prepare for the possibility of inclement weather, drops in temperature, or other life-altering circumstances. An awareness of regional weather patterns is a key component of successful wildlife observation. Animal activity can also spike after weather events have cleared.

Invisibility

Invisibility primarily involves preventing the animals in your vicinity from being aware of your presence. It is first and foremost a state of mind: slow down, be quiet, and remember to appreciate the journey, not just focus on the destination. These vital rules are often overlooked. Consider the simple crunch of leaf litter on the forest floor as a person walks through a habitat. Such a disturbance radiates outward and may impact animals that aren't even in your immediate trajectory.

I spotted this mink after it moved within the branches of a downed willow tree that had fallen into a pond. Mink are generally very active animals that are also excellent observers, hiding in the shadows of rock piles and vegetation while they assess their surroundings.

Of course, there's a lot more to consider when it comes to practicing the art of invisibility. And how you choose to meld with the landscape has tremendous implications in terms of your ability to observe wildlife.

Camouflage

Unlike humans, many species are equipped with the gift of natural camouflage. Seldom in the animal kingdom is the element of disguise more striking than in the contrast in markings between the male and female wood duck. While the drake's iridescent crest and piercing red eyes broadcast its presence, the female's comparatively drab plumage enables it to fade into the landscape and offers protection when nesting. Herein lies an important lesson about the art of concealment—to go unseen helps ensure survival.

So how can you, as an observer, become more skilled in the practice of camouflage? Start by making judicious use of shadows and variety in the landscape; use the local cover to blend in. Review the clothing and gear list in Chapter 1 for practical ways of promoting invisibility. Wear clothing that breaks up your silhouette. I am a big fan of wool clothing. It is quiet, tends not to hold scents, and usually can be found in dull plaids, muted colors, and a variety of camouflage patterns. In warmer seasons you can even cover yourself with mud, clay, charcoal, or ash, yielding a mottled effect. (Solid colors are virtually nonexistent in nature and will only serve to announce your whereabouts.)

Eddie Starnater, director of programming and head instructor of Practical Primitive, has elevated natural camouflage to a high art. In his DVD *Principles of Natural Camouflage: The Science of Invisibility*, he shares the secrets of using natural materials and the surrounding environment to go unseen. He also discusses how the mind perceives and interprets its surroundings. In Starnater's Dead Space class, I learned how the eye is drawn to focal points in the landscape. What is left behind and often overlooked is called dead space. This knowledge, coupled with mindfully applied natural camouflage, can enable you to virtually disappear like a skilled magician. In Starnater's film, it is difficult if not impossible to locate those hidden in each scene once they've vanished into the landscape.

It's important to note that while dressing in dull, earth-based patterns can be helpful, camouflage is generally ineffective if you don't slow down and stay quiet. You could wear the latest and greatest camouflage outfit, but it would not work if you moved quickly and were loud. In fact, many, if not most, of the times I have had close encounters with wildlife, I have been wearing nothing special. Often, I am able to use good cover, but even if I can't, I remain undetected because I am still and quiet. Many hunters, either by law or by choice, wear blaze orange during the big game season without seeming detriment to their quest. So if you're in an area where hunters may be present, it can't hurt to either wear some blaze orange or attach some to a backpack. In finding wildlife, being quiet and still is more important than what you wear.

De-scenting

Another advantage of using natural cover is that it helps conceal human odors. If you choose not to cover yourself with clay, mud, or other forest debris, I would encourage you to take some time to de-scent. Shower with an unscented soap or a naturally fragranced soap such as Dr. Bronner's castile soap. Deodorants, if used, should be unscented. Also pay attention to your diet and determine if this affects your odor. When I haven't taken the time to mask my scent, I've often had shifting breezes reveal my location. Being detected happens even to the most experienced outdoorspersons and to wild predators alike. View it not as failure but an opportunity to learn.

To de-scent my clothing, I first wash out my washing machine with baking soda and hot water. Then I wash my clothes in baking soda and hang them up outside in a natural area away from any human-made odors such as propane fuel (think summer grilling).

Next, I gather all manner of field and forest debris—including goldenrod, mint, apple peelings, dried leaves, pine needles, and rose hips—to make a vat of de-scenting tea. I heat up enough water to fill a container large enough for the clothes I want to treat, add my woodsy mix, and let it brew for half an hour. Then I add my clothing and let it sit overnight. (Keep in mind that certain ingredients, such as blueberries and walnuts, will dye your clothing.) I once again hang these clothes outside to dry, then store them in a plastic or wooden container filled with dry leaves.

I find that taking the time to de-scent is vital to my success. Keeping tabs on wind direction can also help you avoid detection, but you never know when the breeze is going to shift or from which direction an unsuspecting animal might emerge. Whenever possible, approach downwind of your intended quarry.

Movement

Knowing how to move through the wilderness is arguably one of the most important skills you can possess. Patient, deliberate movement translates to not being seen and heard while seeing and hearing all the subtleties in any environment. An intimate knowledge of stealth walking techniques will reward you with experiences you may have felt were previously beyond reach.

Fox Walking

Indigenous people who still live a hunter-gatherer existence walk through the world in a manner different from the typical contemporary city or suburban dweller. By observing predators such as bobcats, foxes, and herons, they learn how to move with fluid grace. These people live in accordance with natural laws, as their ancestors did. They move deliberately with the intention of first infiltrating a landscape and then, once an animal is identified, shifting into stealth mode to close the distance. Fox walking, as this way of moving is called, was once the natural way all people moved about. Changes in lifestyle or worldview likely shifted our gait to what it is today, a weight-forward walk that is noisier, faster, more easily detected, and likely more taxing on the body.

I learned fox walking at Tom Brown Jr.'s Tracker School. Substitute it for your normal, "modernized" gait. If you do it properly, it will enable you to see more clearly, reduce disturbances, and become more highly attuned to your surroundings. Remember, too, that minimizing

Instructions for Fox Walking and Stealth Walking

How rapidly or slowly you move will be a decision you make based on current environmental factors. Both fox walking and stealth walking are best done barefoot or in soft shoes.

FOX WALKING. Slower than a normal modern gait, the fox walk helps a person to slow down, become more aware, and stay quiet. You can still be seen by wildlife when you are moving in this way, but you should be able to detect things sooner than you otherwise would.

- Keep your eyes mostly up so they can quietly scan the environment.
- Use wide-angle vision (see "Sight" in the next chapter).
- Keep a nice, tall posture.
- As you move forward, remain balanced on your back foot and slowly bring your front foot forward.
- Lower your foot to the ground slowly and deliberately.
- As your foot comes down to meet the earth, the outside edge of your foot will come into contact first. Don't put weight on it until you have a sense of what's underfoot. Slowly flatten your foot.

Once you detect an animal you want to move closer to, you can shift to stealth walking.

STEALTH WALKING. This kind of movement is very slow and will test your balance. Think of holding your body like a cat or a heron if it helps you. With time it will feel very natural and lead you to some incredible experiences.

- Keep your eyes mostly up so they can quietly scan the environment.
- Use wide-angle vision.
- As you move forward, lift your foot higher than you do with the fox walk and remain balanced on your back foot.
- Take about a full minute to bring your foot from its back position to the front position. For practice, you can time yourself, but moving

at a slow and invisible speed will come naturally with a little practice

- As your foot comes down to meet the earth, the outside edge of your foot will come into contact first. Slowly flatten your foot.

While stealth walking, it is important that your feet—not your eyes—tell you what's on the ground. This isn't to say you should never glance down, but this should be an exception. Stealth walking can close the gap between you and an animal, so your ability to move your head freely becomes limited. Take stock of your environment. Remember to shift your weight from your back foot to your front foot only when you know it will make little or no noise. Be prepared to alter your step if you come down on something (such as a fragile twig) that might make a sound. Such errors will prove costly.

If executed properly, stealth walking can grant you unbelievably close access to wildlife. Be sure to exercise caution to avoid placing yourself in a situation where you could suffer injury, either from the landscape or unsuspecting prey. Keep in mind, too, there may be times when crawling on your hands and knees or gently sliding across the ground on your stomach is the best course of action. On many occasions I've moved so carefully that I've been rewarded with the opportunity to slowly reach out and touch an animal. When done correctly, you can do this and remain undetected even as you move away.

If you think stealth walking is beyond your capacity to perform, think again. We are all born with a predisposition toward such skills. If you're observing animals that are in a state of contentment—feeding, grooming, or basking—you can rest assured you're on the right track. Again, it's all about not giving the animal's senses anything to detect.

Remain open to each experience. It is not uncommon for me to go out in search of one thing only to come across something unexpected and amazing, like a wood turtle, a hidden fawn, or a bird that is new to me. Often, because I'm being slow and quiet, I find myself having stepped outside of cover, thinking I'm alone, only to see an animal that is also being slow and deliberate. Essentially, I'm invisible even without cover.

One fall afternoon I was making my way along an abandoned railroad bed when I came upon an unexpected traveler. Armed with my camera, I'd hoped to snap a few pictures of some deer foraging on the edge of a nearby wetland. But just as I had steadied my lens, I heard the snap of a twig to the left of the trail. I couldn't tell what it was. I thought it might be a woodchuck, but its body was far too sleek. And it was too big to be a mink. Then my mind flashed with recognition. It was a fisher! I had stealth walked in so quietly that it had no idea I was there. As it passed by me just five feet away, I shifted my weight and inadvertently disturbed some pebbles beneath my feet. The fisher heard me, bounded over a fallen tree, and was gone.

As you move, you should always be thinking, How am I impacting my environment? Being painfully slow and quiet is crucial. And by quiet, I mean *as silent as you can be.* Being as silent as you can be may mean you make some sound. Be mindful, check in with the world around you, and make sure you are not being noticed. Remember that rhythmic sound, such as the pattern of someone walking, is far more noticeable than the occasional subtle crunch. Also, exit any encounter as quietly as you entered.

There are two good reasons for leaving an encounter quietly and carefully. To start with, an animal may have had a hint that someone or something was nearby—perhaps a leaf crunched and you had to wait a few minutes for the animal to relax—and if you simply get up and go without stealth when you are done, you will confirm the animal's concern and make your next attempt at getting close to that individual that much harder. The second reason is one of simple respect. Why not try and remain invisible so as to not add any undue stress to that animal's life?

arm and hand movements will further aid you in masking your presence as you negotiate the wilderness. In more temperate climates, fox walking should be practiced in bare feet or soft-soled footwear, such as moccasins.

When moving through any natural landscape with the goal of seeing and sensing wildlife, it is paramount that you pause, scan, and look. This slow, constant process of stopping, waiting, remaining still, and assessing your environment is a vital ritual.

To practice fox walking, keep your body centered over your hips and take measured and purposeful steps. Pause midway to check your

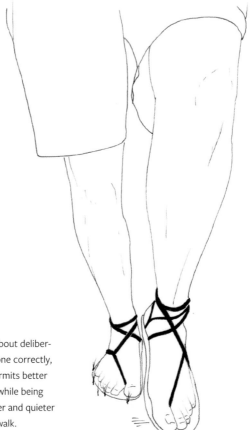

Fox walking is all about deliberate movement. Done correctly, this movement permits better use of the senses while being considerably slower and quieter than the modern walk.

This photo of a chipmunk raises more than a few questions: Will the leaves be used to insulate a nest? How did it end up with a tear in its ear? Was it from a close call with a predator or perhaps a territorial dispute with another chipmunk? Close observation over time can lead to answers to questions like these.

balance if necessary. When your front foot comes down, its outside ridge should quietly meet the forest floor. Take care not to place any weight on this front foot. Now, slowly flatten your sole to gather some impression of what's underfoot.

Ask yourself, Am I going to make much noise if I shift my weight forward? If not, slowly transfer your weight from your back foot to your front. This motion should be smooth and intentional. Remain vigilant and make use of your peripheral vision. Be sure to constantly

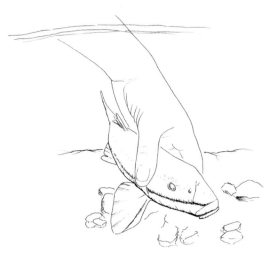

The lessons of fox walking and invisibility can allow the patient naturalist to go unseen and get incredibly close to wildlife. The act of hand fishing is an ancient technique that has been practiced around the world.

survey your environment. This may sound easy, but for many people it is not. Being slow and quiet can be painfully challenging for some. Stick with it. This most basic of tasks is vital to your success and is well worth the investment in the time required to perfect it. As you traverse the landscape, presume animals are everywhere and the slightest misstep will betray your location.

Writing this book made me reflect on my skills and how I use them for consistent success in pursuing close encounters with wildlife. When I enter a landscape with the intent of seeing and not disturbing its residents, I emulate a predatory animal. I open my senses, soak in what is in front of me with my eyes and ears, take a few steps, look, look some more, soak in the sounds, broaden my vision, and move a step or two more. I repeat this process over and over. When I spot an animal or bird I want to get closer to, I use the landscape and trees to my advantage and very often move into a full-out stalk. I take advantage of wind gusts to help cover the sound of my movement through the trees and grasses.

My first serious attempt at stealth movement took place in my early twenties when I ventured into a meadow near the local golf course by my parents' home in suburban Buffalo, New York. I presented myself with the simple challenge of making as little noise as possible. I removed my shoes so I could feel the earth beneath my feet and took care not to step on any brittle leaf litter gathered along the field edge. I shifted to my hands and knees to make my way through a dense thicket. I was moving so slowly and quietly that an eastern cottontail hopped out in front of me. I had never been in such close proximity to a wild animal before. I could see that she was eating clover. She showed no signs of alarm.

Twenty minutes later, after I had moved fifty or so yards, the thicket opened up into an immature stand of aspens and I was able to return to my feet. Several white-tailed deer suddenly appeared on the opposite side of the small grove. It happened so quickly I didn't have time to respond; a doe and her two fawns stood less than twenty yards away from me. As the wind shifted, they moved on, not trusting the situation.

I came to a large sugar maple that was perfectly suited for climbing. I found a comfortable spot to rest on a bough, and not ten minutes later a fox emerged from a tangle of grapevines below. Like the rabbit, the fox showed no signs of concern and casually went about grooming its thick coat.

Fox walking in and of itself does not guarantee invisibility. It simply helps to ensure your movement is less apparent.

Stealth Walking

Fox walking is slow, deliberate movement with much more consideration than our modern gait. But even while employing it, you can still be detected if you are not moving slowly enough. Stealth walking, on the other hand, allows you to move without being seen. Stealth walking is a natural extension of fox walking, like shifting gears from a padding step to a creep. It is painfully, excruciatingly slow. In fact, one full step can (and in many cases should) take longer than a minute.

Like fox walking, the skill of stealth walking was introduced to me through the Tracker School. (They call it stalking, or at least they did. Nowadays that word has taken on so many negative connotations that replacing it with stealth walking just avoids misunderstanding.) When I think of stealth walking, I envision a chameleon moving so slowly that its unsuspecting prey has no idea it's being hunted. When stealth walking, it may help to mimic a long-legged wading bird like the great blue heron.

Challenging Circumstances

Every so often you will encounter difficult circumstances that will make being stealthy even more challenging. Leaves that were once damp and are now frozen, crusty snow, gravelly places, or dry leaves coupled with no wind can make being quiet more difficult. There are several ways to approach these situations:

- Keep at it and just go even more slowly. Be extra vigilant about not creating rhythms of sound. Look for logs and rocks that can be used as walkways to help reduce noise.
- Forget about being quiet and just get out to a promising site early and then settle in. (See "Sitting" below.)
- Try to sound like a wild animal. I have mimicked the sounds of the relatively loud gray squirrel as it moves and forages on the forest floor. I generally use this technique in very dry leaves when I want to move a short distance.

Sitting

Then again, why not hang out and let wildlife come to you? When you're sitting or standing you're likely not making any sound and should also be making little to no movement. This method of viewing animals, whereby you emulate the world's most efficient predators, is a favorite of mine. And far from propagating a sense of isolation, sitting alone will paradoxically *increase* your connection with the outdoors.

Beyond being an effective tactic, finding a place to be stationary is likely going to be the best choice in places where difficult ground cover makes being silent very challenging. For example, where crusted snow makes being perfectly quiet almost impossible, one strategy is to get

How to Be Still

For some people, being still can be challenging. Here are some suggestions:

- Leave distractions at home. (Bring your phone with you for safety reasons but leave it off unless you truly need it.)
- Give yourself the gift of time.
- Being still doesn't necessarily mean being "frozen." As long as your movements are slow and mindful doing something natural with your hands like carving a stick or making cordage from dried grasses can help quiet your mind. You can also draw things that you see such as tracks, flowers, birds, or animals.
- Move very slowly (if you feel you should move) and use wide-angle vision. (See "Sight" in Chapter 3.)

Dan Erickson blogs about simple living and mindfulness. He has some excellent suggestions on how to be still on his web page at hipdiggs .com/being-still/. He writes, "In all of these methods of being still, there is one universal truth: you need to let go of all the internal and external distractions. Distractions may still be present, and you may be acutely aware of everything going on, but you reach a point of detachment. You gain the ability to be still in the midst of the distractions. You are aware and alert, but not worried, anxious, or consumed by anything other than your present stillness of mind."

outside early, move comparatively quickly to a promising spot to view wildlife, and then just settle in.

Blinds, or methods of cover, can make it easier for you to be invisible to wildlife while you sit and wait. These need not be elaborate—a simple brush pile will do wonders to break up the silhouette of the human form. The trick with blinds is to either use a natural blind or to set one up well before you're planning to use it; the wildlife in your area will need time to adjust to any additions to the landscape.

One autumn, I regularly bow hunted in the woods behind my home using an old cherry tree as a blind. I realized it was also an excellent perch for simply watching my local wildlife. This tree had a large section of bark hanging from the main trunk. Using this and the small hillside behind me, I was able to effectively break up my outline. One day I had several deer venture within range, a gray squirrel perch on my boot, and a gray fox walk within several feet of my person. Not bad for a few hours of bow hunting from the ground!

Tree stands—open or closed platforms secured in a tree—are also a wonderful vehicle for viewing animals and offer distinct advantages over being on the ground. The first is that if you haven't properly de-scented, your odor may be carried away without incident. Second, many animals aren't used to looking toward the sky for predators. Not only do tree stands offer the benefit of a new, contrasting perspective, but they can also render you far less conspicuous.

Although I love climbing trees, I encourage the use of modern safety equipment. Be sure to exercise care when using tree stands. Use a manufactured stand and be sure to follow all safety guidelines. Every year people who haven't taken the time to read the instructions fall out of tree stands, resulting in injury or death.

Exercises

- Keep a journal of your forays into the wild, noting the weather, temperature, season, and type of ecosystem. Do certain animals favor particular conditions, locations, or times of day? If so, why?

- Observe wildlife from several different perspectives. Spend time on foot, on your stomach, and in trees. Does one vantage point afford you greater benefits than others for some species?

- Practice stealth walking with and without footwear, and with different types of footwear. Are there distinct advantages to walking barefoot? If walking in snow, are certain types of footwear more conducive to staying quiet? Challenge yourself to be as quiet as possible.

- For many people, both balancing and holding still can be difficult when learning to fox walk and stealth walk. A slackline (essentially a backyard tightrope) can be beneficial. I always find that after I practice with the slackline and regain my ability to walk the line without a spotter, I am stronger and much more able to hold in almost any position while walking on solid ground.

- Practice hiding with kids and adults alike. One game I like is called Camouflage. One person chooses a spot to stand and closes their eyes for several minutes while everyone uses the landscape to conceal themselves. Each hider must be able to see the person who is "it." Then the seeker announces that they are opening their eyes and begins to look. They can turn around but cannot move from their spot. If someone is seen they are called in. After several minutes, anyone left hiding is given the chance to move closer and hide again.

CHAPTER 3

Use of the Senses

As awareness grows, appreciation grows too.
As appreciation grows, so does empathy.

—JON YOUNG, *WHAT THE ROBIN KNOWS: HOW BIRDS*
REVEAL THE SECRETS OF THE NATURAL WORLD

Years ago my friend Tim Drake and I co-led a tracking workshop during our weekly Primitive Pursuits program with a group of middle school students. As we practiced new skills and followed a set of deer tracks through a hemlock forest, a disturbance drew our attention—the alarms of a murder (flock) of crows. It is often difficult to discern what crows are attempting to communicate, but in this case their meaning was clear. Tim and I checked in with each other and agreed about the source of the concern.

"What do you think these crows are telling us?" we asked the group. "They seem to be exerting a great deal of energy." This question prompted the students to pay attention to the crows' activity.

We encouraged the group to remain alert, move slowly, and pause to see if they could reach an understanding of the situation. As we moved closer we noted that it was indeed crows, and only crows, that appeared distressed. Their actions and calls were intense and powerful.

Tim and I led the group past a small pond and into a hardwood forest marked with a few tall white pines. When we paused, we could see crows swooping down at great speed in a pendulum-like curve, their efforts directed toward the top of the tallest pine. As we stood and observed, we could see that our hunch was correct.

A great horned owl was perched high among the branches, and the crows, disturbed by its presence, were making every effort to drive it out of the woods. The two species are fierce adversaries; I have seen owl pellets consisting of almost nothing but crow bones and feathers.

This was the first time most of our participants had ever seen a great horned owl. Our students learned a valuable lesson that day: always keep your senses attuned, and above all, ask questions and be curious.

As your understanding of the natural world develops, you will come to increasingly rely on instinct grounded in past experience. Invisibility will enable you to quietly enter natural landscapes and assume the role of observer, and then your senses will alert you to the presence of animals. This heightened level of observation is achieved by honing your sight, hearing, smell, and touch, your primary aids when it comes to wildlife awareness.

Sight

Sight is our dominant sense. For those of us with unimpaired vision, roughly 80 percent of the information we process comes through our eyes. Using your vision to its fullest extent is, therefore, of paramount importance. In the modern world we are often required to look directly at objects such as computer screens, digital devices, and televisions. But in the natural world, we need more than singular focus; instead we need to pick up visual information from the greater expanse around us.

PREVIOUS IMAGE It is often the alarming of crows that draws my attention to a nearby hawk or owl, such as this great horned owl. (iStock/BirdImages)

A few years back, I was picking my way through a forest in search of a white-tailed buck I was hoping to photograph. I moved like a bobcat, moving ahead a few deliberate steps and then stopping to survey the environment. Each advance brought new layers of perspective into focus. As I scanned and made my way, I watched the birds and chipmunks. My woodland allies were telling me there were no predators afoot. My mind was on deer, which have a remarkable talent for fading into the landscape. (I have, on more than one occasion, come upon bedding deer, always grateful for my success but also amazed I didn't spot them sooner.)

It was late September, a time when deciduous trees shed their leaves and offer views into the pre-rut activity of multiple young males. In the past it hadn't been unusual for me to see as many as seven bucks at one time in this semi-urban wood. But this year my quarry, the dominant buck, was having none of it; these were *his* woods. With each step I paused and scanned. Then something, a subtle movement, caught my peripheral vision. An ear twitched, and a rack of ten points emerged. A downed tree concealed his head and body as he rested in the leaves. I moved closer, aware of my impact on the forest. I hoped to remain a benign force. As my vantage on the buck improved, I confirmed it was my old friend, HO2. (This particular deer was part of a suburban study and that was the identifier on his ear tags.)

Despite his apparent comfort hiding in the shadows amidst civilization, I had learned that one misstep would usually send him crashing through the forest. I was fortunate this day and did not prompt him to flee. Instead, I was rewarded with an extended viewing opportunity and some wonderful photographs. Because I had been fox walking, my eyes had been free to scan the landscape.

Take a moment to experiment with softening your gaze. First, put yourself in a promising place to observe the natural world, such as the edge of a field, wetland, or open woods. With your fingers and thumbs extended, hold your hands up and out to the sides of your face, one hand to the left and one to the right, as if you were looking through a window. Gaze directly through your hands, keeping each fully in your peripheral vision. Now slowly move your hands outward to the point

To utilize wide-angle vision, place your hands up as if you are looking through a window. Pay equal attention to both hands. Slowly spread your hands apart. When they get to the periphery of your vision, wiggle your fingers. At this point you should discover that your vision has "softened" and has become more sensitized to movement.

that they reach the edge of your periphery. If your hands become difficult to see, wiggle your fingers.

If you do this properly, you will notice that you are not focused on any one thing. What you've done has softened your vision and sensitized your eyes. At this point you should be able to notice many things at once. For example, you might notice the flick of a songbird, a foraging chipmunk, or the rustling of leaves all in the same moment.

Spend time practicing this skill, paying attention to the things that enter your field of vision but keeping your eyes trained on the bigger picture. This is another vital tool I learned while attending the Tracker School. Tom Brown Jr. calls this skill wide-angle vision, and naturalist Jon Young refers to it as owl eyes. To adopt a more limited viewpoint is to willingly compromise your experience. This kind of vision can be balanced with more focused vision. If something catches your attention, simply focus your attention, identify, and then shift back into owl eyes.

I have always found it valuable to alter my perspective and question what it is I'm seeing, all the while noting subtle changes in the landscape—rippling bodies of water, trembling branches, twitching grasses or sedges. Be the skeptic when observing—question assumptions, scrutinize all possibilities, wait, listen, and look. Everything I do is informed by experience. I often train my eyes on the edge of a transition area and then soften my vision in an attempt to detect patterns or movement.

Learning to be patient and staying in the moment are critical. Give your senses time to soak up all that is in front of you. Very often when I'm looking at a woodpile at home, for example, I see nothing at first glance. In a short time, though, I start to notice the garter snakes that frequent these spots and are hidden in the shadows.

It's important to maintain awareness of all the animals in your vicinity. If you're paying attention only to the species you're attempting to approach, you could easily startle or push the boundaries of personal space of another creature, breaking its baseline and causing it to send out an alarm or distress call, alerting the entire area to your presence.

Hearing

The extent to which you experience the natural world is enhanced not only by the sounds you hear but also by your interpretation of those sounds. There are fundamental causes for the noises that animals make. Unlike humans, animals rarely (if ever) have time to engage in mindless chatter. Close listening will aid patient naturalists in unraveling the ongoing mysteries to which they bear witness.

Each year with great anticipation I look forward to the seasonal courtship ritual of the timberdoodle, or American woodcock. When not migrating, this well-camouflaged bird spends most of its time in fields and moist woodlands. With eyes positioned high on its head, the woodcock can easily identify potential dangers as it forages for

Spring peepers are masters of disguise. These tiny yet boisterous frogs can be challenging to spot even as they vocalize just a few feet away.

earthworms in the soil. Its mottled plumage makes it very difficult to spot when it is not moving.

The male woodcock initiates his mating ritual at both dawn and dusk. He begins by claiming an open area known as a singing ground and emitting a "peent" call—a distinctive, comical blurt. This is followed by a dramatic display in which he flies up into the sky in a wide, spiraling arc. At the apex of his flight, he then makes a rapid, zigzagging descent. This results in a high-pitched twittering sound produced by air rushing through the bird's primary feathers.

It was during this peculiar dance one spring that I took advantage of the brief time the bird was in flight to capture some photographs. With each aerial burst I crept closer, only a yard or two at a time, hoping to approximate where the bird might land. More than once, this chunky "grapefruit with wings" zipped past my head, landing only a few feet away. The bird never detected me, and as a result I was granted close access to this bizarre yet fascinating seasonal display.

I always attempt to listen with an unbiased ear when I'm out in the woods, searching for patterns such as the drumming of woodpeckers, the alarming of crows, or the subtle movement of deer (as opposed to the not-so-subtle sounds of gray squirrels). Because of the immense range of sounds nature produces, at times this can feel a bit overwhelming. I often begin with two basic questions:

1. What kind of animal is making this noise?
2. Is the animal I'm listening to acting in a way that supports life, or is it concerned for its safety?

If you hear an animal giving a distress call, first, determine whether you are the cause. If so, this is the time to learn why and what you can do better next time to avoid detection. If, however, something else appears to have provoked the distress call, be the proverbial fly on the wall and quietly observe the constant drama unfolding in the natural world.

Determining the origin of a sound can be much like seeing the animal itself; many ornithologists are able to "bird by ear," that is, identify the species by its unique call. Unidentified sounds, however, are sometimes the most captivating.

Once in early spring while I was leading a group on an overnight outing through eighteen inches of snow, we stopped at a spring to collect water. While filling our bottles, we heard a faint, odd sound slip from beneath the historic stonework. The sound stopped but then resumed a few moments later. We listened and waited. Although we never determined the sound's origin, it was clear that something, most likely a frog, was awakening from its winter slumber.

Don't ignore sounds that aren't produced by animals. All manner of sounds can teach us something about the world and how all things are interrelated. Perhaps the wind has picked up, and a storm is moving in. Events such as these will influence the choices animals make. Patterns will soon emerge. In short, don't ignore *anything*.

Groundhogs, or woodchucks as they are commonly known, are related to marmots. Their range extends from central Alaska through much of Canada and deep into the southern United States. Groundhogs are not fast runners; hence, they are on constant alert and rarely venture far from the safety of their den. (iStock/shaunl)

Smell

For a good portion of my life, my sense of smell was very poor; I could detect only the most potent of odors. But after I changed to a more primal-based diet of mostly vegetables, fruits, nuts, and meats (I say mostly because I still find it hard to resist my son's homemade chocolate chip cookies), my sense of smell came back, and I have never since taken it for granted. Even supposedly dreadful smells, such as skunk spray and urine, are now welcome.

The ability we have to detect certain scents pales in comparison to the scent-detection abilities of many of our counterparts in the animal kingdom, but this doesn't mean we shouldn't make use of this skill. I find that closing my eyes helps me focus on smells (and sounds). Over the years I have encouraged my students to employ their sense of smell by blindfolding them while they are spread out in a natural area, and instructing them to find a second instructor by following the scent of a smoldering tinder fungus he is holding.

Once while I was tracking in patchy snow, I came across a set of red fox prints. As I followed the tracks, I began to notice a pungent odor. The fox had been marking his territory, and I soon found his scent easier to follow than the footprints themselves! Aided by a light breeze, one scent post led me to another. As I worked my way through the forest, I walked up and off an old logging road and into a thicket, where I located the fox's den.

Touch

Touch is a critical and often underused component of outdoor awareness. Coming into contact with plants and trees as I negotiate the wilderness provides constant sensory input. In many ways, calmly reaching out and touching an animal without its knowledge is the ultimate test of one's skills.

One of my first experiences of coming into contact with a wild animal occurred in the backyard of a house where my wife and I were renting an apartment. My target wasn't especially cunning, fast, or well-equipped to evade predation. It was a groundhog that I spotted from our kitchen window. This rodent, like many of its kind, stayed close to its den in case it needed to seek cover. Woodchucks may not be swift, but they're built like tanks—sturdy and stout with a low center of gravity. They have poor eyesight and only average hearing.

I began my pursuit even before I opened the door leading down the back stairs to the yard, knowing that one small misstep would foil my efforts. I kept a watchful and deliberate eye on my quarry. It took me twenty minutes to make my way down the stairs and into the grass. This property was on a hill that had been terraced, and the woodchuck was below the house on the first plateau, feasting on clover and dandelion. With my attention focused, I made my way across the lawn, creeping ever closer. I spanned a gap of forty feet over the course of forty-five minutes.

During this time the woodchuck occasionally paused, looked up, and sat upright to survey the environment. Sometimes he'd turn toward me and continue foraging, but at no point did he make note of my presence. As I neared a swing set I gently lowered myself into a crawling position and came within arm's reach. At this point he had his butt end to me and was feeding contentedly. As I reached toward him, he shifted backward and my fingers came into contact with the coarse hairs of his hindquarters. He was completely unaware of me. I was amazed by, and grateful for, this experience. After a few moments I turned around and, with equal care, made my way back to the house.

Changing Your Perspective

In addition to sharpening your senses, you will want to consider changes in perspective. This can take myriad forms—walking a trail from a different direction, getting off your feet and onto all fours or your stomach, exploring places at different times of day, taking time to investigate the small spaces found around logs and rocks. This will force you to use your senses in new or forgotten ways.

Ideally you will combine the skills introduced here in a fluid, cohesive manner, and use each concept appropriately as specific circumstances arise. Some senses will take precedence over others, depending on the situation. If I'm near a waterfall or in the presence of other natural phenomena (such as wind) that produce white noise, I may lean more heavily on my vision. Conversely, if I'm out at dusk and visibility is poor, I will rely more on my ears. But my experiences, ultimately, are an amalgam of all of my senses—a fusion of my ability to perceive the natural environment as a whole.

Using Sight and Hearing to Identify a New Animal

Identifying a new species can be an incredibly rewarding pursuit. Author and ornitholgist Dr. Steve Kress teaches about the six categories of inquiry designed to help birders narrow down their choices and home in on the new species they have observed. The categories are body shape, behavior, body size, field marks, song, and habitat. By observing and asking questions related to these six areas of inquiry, you will find that identifying new birds becomes easier and more natural as time goes by and experience is gained.

Body shape helps to narrow down your choices to a family of birds. A wren, for example, has a shape very different from a downy woodpecker.

Behavior refers to movements, flight patterns, and eating or hunting techniques that are unique to a given species.

Body size is most meaningful if you compare what you are seeing to a bird you already know. For example, Is this bird I'm observing bigger or smaller than a robin?

Field marks refer to the particular colors and patterns you can easily see.

Song is distinctive enough that once learned, the song of a particular species is generally enough to make a proper identification with.

Habitat can help to narrow your choices, especially during the breeding season. A great blue heron, for example, is generally seen standing in or near water, although it sometimes hunts for insects and mice in a field. It is important to remember that some species very much correlate with a specific habitat ("indicator" species) while other species can be found in a variety of habitats ("non-indicator" species.) Horned larks, for example, are indicators of prairies and open fields. Great horned owls, in contrast, are quite adaptable and can be spotted in a variety of habitats, including forests, open country, golf courses, and even cities.

These same categories of inquiry can be used with any other area of wildlife identification, whether it be reptiles and amphibians, fish, insects, or mammals.

On a paddle trip several years ago, I spotted what looked a bit like a fisher swimming across a narrow stretch of river. The animal was backlit, so seeing any coloring was difficult, but it appeared to me to be a mustelid (a member of the family that includes weasels, badgers, otters, ferrets, minks, and wolverines). When it got to the bank and exited the water, it shook for a moment and looked a bit like a bottle brush with its hair sticking up. It then disappeared into the alders. I wasn't sure what I had seen. It was too small to be an otter and too big to be a mink. Fisher didn't seem right either, and as I came to learn, I was too far north of typical fisher habitat.

Several days later I spent time with a wonderful couple, and they suggested marten. That was it! I hadn't seen a marten in many years, and it just hadn't entered my thoughts. The size and shape was right, and the fact that it wasn't sleek when it came out of the water helped me feel confident that I had spotted a marten. When I have seen otter and mink, which are very aquacentric mammals, they are comparatively always slick and smooth when they exit the water. This marten's fur, on the other hand, looked more like that of a wet dog who had just shaken off the excess after a good swim.

Exercises

○ Identify a location where you can sit and observe the comings and goings of wildlife. Do this at different times of the day and use your senses to note changes, if any, in baseline.

○ Hike a familiar trail from a different direction or a different perspective (or better yet, get off the trail and wander, if that is permissible). Experiment with crawling on your hands and knees instead of walking.

○ Collect examples of different natural odors—a branch of white pine, a walnut, a stem of mint leaves. Then, while sitting at a table, blindfold yourself and explore each through touch and smell. Describe these objects in terms of their texture and odor. Come to know them not by their given name but by their unique characteristics.

○ Discover and seek to identify a sound. Often you will hear a sound that is difficult to identify. Be patient and try your best to find the source based on the clues you can discover.

CHAPTER 4

Animal Language and Behavior

Write me how many notes there be
In the new Robin's ecstasy
Among astonished boughs

—EMILY DICKINSON, FROM "BRING ME THE
SUNSET IN A CUP"

One summer, a gray fox began visiting my yard each evening around dusk. As my wife and I sat by the window, we watched what seemed to be the most erratic, confounding behavior. The fox would sit for a moment and then pounce into the grass. Sit, wait, and pounce. I observed no mice, rabbits, or other prey species that seemed enticing. My wife wondered if it was ill with rabies.

The fox's behavior continued for days unabated until my curiosity got the better of me and I decided to get closer one evening to try to unravel the mystery. Following an easy approach around the south side of the house, I began the painfully slow stalk across open lawn toward some hay bales I was using as an archery target.

It took me more than an hour to reach the bales, at which point I sat down. All the while, the fox had been working the north side of the yard and was now headed in my direction. Sit, wait, and pounce. Sit, wait, and pounce. Over and over again she repeated this odd ritual. I could see that she wasn't rabid and that her coat was well groomed, so the reasons for her behavior were not yet clear.

I became increasingly nervous as she approached, worried she might sense me and disappear into the thicket. But when she came within ten feet of me, I finally had my answer. Beetles! Beetles were hatching from the lawn and the fox was gobbling them up. This was something I had never heard of or seen before, but here it was, happening right in front of me. The fox never noticed me and was later drawn away by the sounds of other insects rising from their burrows.

The next evening, I observed this same fox hunting on one end of the yard for beetles while an eastern cottontail calmly munched clover on the adjoining hillside. I was convinced she was aware of the rabbit but chose to focus instead on the more easily captured insects. Later that summer, I came across fox scat filled with beetle casings.

The fundamental questions of what an animal is doing and why follow naturally from observing behavior such as that of my gray fox. These questions can be answered by *interpreting what you see* based on the context, time of year, and your knowledge of instinctual needs. A detailed understanding and interpretation of animal language and behavior will equip you to understand an animal's motivations.

The following pages introduce you to basic concepts that lay the foundation for a more in-depth study of what motivates and influences animal conduct. We'll begin with the primary governing agent—the

PREVIOUS SPREAD Gray fox habitat stretches from southern Canada to northern Venezuela, and covers a large portion of the United States. Gray foxes prefer somewhat wilder habitats than the red fox but still may be found in woodlots that border suburban areas. (Melissa Groo)

rule of energy conservation. Then you will learn how to catalog behaviors in an organized inventory known as an ethogram. You can use this tool to predict behaviors of specific animals you may have observed or hope to observe.

The Rule of Energy Conservation

Wild animals work on a lean energy budget. They use the energy they possess in sensible ways and for the most part don't squander it on play. (There are, of course, exceptions to this rule. Otters, dolphins, and ravens, for example, play throughout their lifespan, and young animals often play as a means of learning the skills of survival.) Making choices that conserve energy is for the most part a universal standard.

This basic piece of natural law will aid you when you think of it this way: if energy is channeled into a behavior, there's likely a good reason for it. Migration, courtship rituals and displays, den excavation, food storage, and avoiding predation all require considerable amounts of energy, but the investment is worth it. In most cases, animals are slaves to economy. Deer won't bound through the forest unless provoked; otherwise their movements are fluid, efficient, and executed in the interest of remaining unseen.

Let's take a moment to look at typical reactions when an animal is faced with danger, with the rule of energy conservation in mind. These are the usual responses of many land-dwelling mammals to a perceived threat, in order from initial response to last resort:

1. Freeze, keep quiet, and gather information in an attempt to identify the potential disturbance. Many animals, particularly prey species, maintain a near-constant state of vigilance.
2. Sneak away. This is a shrewd tactic in that it is more energy efficient than running and involves fewer risks. Such a response will minimize the threat of injury and is more likely to enable an animal to remain undetected.
3. Flee. This act, which happens after an animal's personal space or safety has been pushed to the brink, is energy intensive and comes with the added risk of exposing its location.

Resting can be a multifunction activity. These turkey vultures, which were drawn to the area because of a large composting facility, may be digesting their food as they bask in the sun.

4. Fight. At this point it should be clear that the basic notion of "fight or flight" is a considerably nuanced concept. As a last resort, an animal may have to turn on a threat, becoming aggressive in an attempt to protect itself or its young from a predator.

Aggression from animals toward humans is rare but can and does happen. These situations include times when a person has gotten too close (for example, when I was charged by the bison), is no longer at the top of the food chain (and is literally being hunted), or is a threat and the animal is simply frightened and trying to protect itself or its young. Being handled or restrained in any way can be a very frightening situation for any animal. It is important to remain empathetic and try to understand the experience from the animal's point of view. The "Guidelines for Thoughtful Engagement" in Chapter 1 will help you turn empathy into respectful action.

This knowledge of basic animal behavior can and should be used to gauge the development of your skills. On one end of the spectrum, the novice may see little or no wildlife. Animals have either fled or snuck away or are in the process of retreating in a state of alarm. (Although, even if you are observing and noticing the radiating disturbances created by concerned wildlife because of something you may have done, this shows you are becoming more attuned as an observer to the world around you. You are now not just moving blindly through the forest, like so many people do; you are starting to recognize your impact on the wildlife around you.) On the other end, a seasoned naturalist will be able to view animals acting in a baseline manner. Over time you will note your improvements in this area, comparing the once-alarmist behaviors of nearby animals to their eventual shift toward baseline behaviors. When you become invisible, you are in a good position to start unraveling the lives of animals and understanding what they are doing.

It should be noted that if an animal appears to be concerned and in a state of information gathering, you may be able to recover from such a situation. If, for example, you've snapped a twig and drawn attention to yourself, the best thing you can do is return the animal's motionless stance and be patient. Ideally, the animal will come to the conclusion that everything's all right and return to a state of relative calm.

Nonmammalian members of the animal kingdom approach evading predation and the rule of energy conservation in different ways. Some reptiles and amphibians are renowned for their autotomy, or ability to jettison and regenerate portions of their bodies. Certain species of lizard and salamander, for example, will "drop" their tails when threatened. The discarded appendage then writhes about, drawing the predator's attention and aiding the animal's escape. Still, most animals (and mammals, in particular) adhere to the freeze—sneak away— flee—fight course of action when responding to environmental dangers.

Thinking Like a Hungry Bear

Before delving into a discussion of animal behavior and the ethogram, it is important to consider the nature of plant-animal relationships. All animals must eat, and the availability of food impacts their activity. Any study of an animal's behavior must begin with (and is inextricably

tied to) that animal's environment—and this requires a familiarity with local flora. (Even a true carnivore is tied to plants through its prey's browse.)

Predicting where an animal might be, based on a food source's abundance or scarcity, is a skill that can only be mastered over time. Part of your journaling process (see Chapter 6) will include recording what an animal eats. Be sure to examine scat for evidence of recent meals and remember to inspect browse for indications of diet.

All animals take advantage of seasonal food availability or larders. After many years of close observation, I have reached a point where I can predict when our local throng of raccoons will emerge for the annual cherry harvest. Knowing the location of these seasonal larders (and which animals are likely to plunder them) will place you in a position to observe wildlife.

In the summer of 2016, I was on an Adirondack canoeing trip with my younger son, Aron. One evening around dusk, we decided to quietly paddle our canoe up a small creek. After passing several beaver lodges, we heard something move in the thicket along the bank. It was a bear.

He was calmly stripping mountain holly berries from their bushes, using his forepaws to pull each branch down to his mouth to feed. It was hard to tell if the bear was aware of our presence; he appeared genuinely unconcerned. This turned out to be one of three bears we observed from our canoe over the course of a half hour.

These animals were clearly drawn to the creek because of the bounty those bushes provided. The more knowledgeable about bears and their foraging habits one becomes, the more common incidents like these become. Because this plant favors moist soils, was in season, and is favored among bears, the chances of an encounter were better than average. Admittedly, we chanced upon this amazing encounter, being unaware at that time that the hollies were in fruit. This

Black bears are incredible animals that can be found in a variety of habitats. Historically, black bears populated most of the United States and Canada.; today, they tend to be found only where adequate forest cover is available. (iStock/through-my-lens)

knowledge is now part of the bank of information I will bring with me into future encounters.

Basic Questions about What You Observe

A deep understanding of animal language and behavior begins with asking some basic yet important questions. The answers to these questions form the foundation of understanding the interplay of all life on Earth. Begin with, What's going on here and why? The answer isn't always obvious. Consider all the possibilities and resist the urge to fill the void with an easy solution.

In my own experience, I can think of innumerable situations where I was unsure of a particular animal's motivations. These mysteries are part of what makes the wild so intriguing. Be aware, though, that there is a difference between knowing, guessing, and inferring. A good example of this is the easily observed communal nesting of crows that takes place from the fall through the winter. One possibility for this behavior is that the crows have found a good spot for off-season roosting and everyone shows up to benefit from the good location. Another motivation might be the safety found in numbers. A third possible explanation is that crows share information that helps with survival. In the absence of conclusive evidence, the best approach is to keep an open mind about possibilities.

Another way to frame basic inquiry is to ask yourself, Am I witnessing a life-supporting behavior or a life-protective or life-defensive behavior? This question builds on the first in that it asks us to consider baseline. Animals have work to do: they forage, build shelter, raise young, groom, and rest. But they also have to remain vigilant so they don't become someone else's meal. Don't neglect to ask questions in this regard, as they may lead to deeper inquiry.

Behaviors to Catalog in an Ethogram

An ethogram is an inventory of the behaviors a particular animal or species exhibits over the course of its annual cycle. A number of scientists, including renowned primatologist Jane Goodall, have made use of this tool. I have used it to understand animal behavior. You can use it, too, by making a list in your journal of the behaviors you observe as you follow a specific animal or type of animal through the year. Asking questions with the ethogram in mind will aid you in making sensible, objective, and concrete hypotheses about the natural world and its inhabitants. From a general standpoint, the more complex and highly developed the organism, the more individualistic its behavior can be. Animals with more primitive nervous systems, however, may also display unique personalities. Garter snakes, for example, show a great variability in temperament. I have handled dozens of garter snakes over the years and have come to recognize those that can be a bit nervous and nippy and those that are comfortable being held. I would caution you about making snap judgments based on the observation of just a few members of a given species.

Following is a discussion of behaviors that comprise a typical ethogram. While it's possible that you may add or remove categories depending on the species in question, the information you gather will be driven in large part by inquiry. It should be noted that some of these behaviors will overlap with one another and may (and very often will) share similar characteristics. The distinctions will be in the details and grounded questioning.

Life Cycle Behaviors

Life cycle behaviors orient themselves around general needs of survival that can be part of daily as well as yearly concerns. They include behaviors having to do with sheltering, ingesting, elimination, self-maintenance, resting, inclement weather strategies, and molting or shedding.

SHELTERING

Each species has its own unique way of taking shelter. Some, like deer, don't seek shelter in the form of a den or nest but know how to position themselves strategically within the landscape to stay out of the weather, as well as to stay aware.

Late one winter while I was working as a naturalist at the Fairview Lake Environmental Education Center in Newton, New Jersey, a group

Nesting is a baseline behavior that requires a considerable amount of effort. For many bird species, such as these starlings, a nest is vital to help ensure future generations. (iStock/ Peter Vahlersvik)

of coworkers and I joined a team of biologists from the state's Division of Fish and Wildlife. As guests, our job was to quietly observe as the biologists followed a radio signal to a hibernating female black bear. This young mother had lost her cubs the previous year, perhaps due to being underweight and not able to produce enough milk for her little ones. Our biologists were hopeful this year they would find a heavier sow with healthy cubs.

We followed the biologists through the forest along the base of the Appalachian escarpment. Immense, car-sized boulders at the base of the hill offered an array of den choices for coyotes, porcupines, and bears. When the signal strengthened, we were asked to wait. The team of professionals left us in the woods as they scrambled up the rocks to locate and anesthetize the bear.

Ten minutes later we received word to rejoin the team. The young mother had been hauled from her den—a space between two large stones near the base of the slope. Although this was an archetypal cavelike bear den, many are not—the first bear I ever saw, in fact, was awakened from its rest beneath the shelter of a large root-ball.

As the biologists collected their data, my group was handed the responsibility of looking after her trio of cubs. The young bears alternated between sleeping and waking, offering plaintive, nasally whines in combination with raspy, harrowing shrieks. Once the biologists finished, the family was carefully tucked back into their den.

Questions to ask when noting sheltering behaviors:

· What does the animal do to meet its nesting needs?
· Where does it go to escape inclement weather or avoid predation?
· Does the animal have casual sheltering or resting spots?
· Does the animal require a special situation for hibernation?

INGESTING

Much of an animal's daily routine revolves around the need to find food while using its limited energy reserves in sensible ways. This need is a constant challenge for all wildlife.

On a trip to the beach one summer I noticed a bird that was new to me. Observing from a distance that didn't seem to intrude upon its space, I watched as this long-legged wader worked its way along, regularly probing the wet sand with its long, curved bill. Every few tries it extracted a small crab. Everything about the design of this bird, which turned out to be a whimbrel, made sense. It was perfectly constructed for a life of foraging along the beach.

It should be noted that ingesting behaviors can vary greatly from one species to the next. Some species hunt while others forage or gather. One dramatic hunting strategy I have observed on numerous occasions is the ambush tactics of urban and suburban Cooper's hawks. From my experience it seems that a surprise ambush is the preferred tactic of these birds as opposed to pursuing flying prey. (Cooper's hawks are accipiters, agile birds of prey that hunt smaller birds.) Knowing where pigeons, starlings, and feeder birds are likely to be, Cooper's hawks glide in low over the rooftops, remaining unseen, and then strike an unsuspecting bird. This dramatic hunting tactic is quite common.

Black bears are generally plant eaters, with animal protein making up only about 15 percent of their diet. In the spring of 2020 my region was in a bit of a drought, and our mostly invisible bear population became quite visible as they searched for food. The drought had made it hard to find good natural forage, so many bears moved toward human sources such as bird feeders, garbage, and unprotected farm feed. A bear was even spotted in one of our city parks near Cayuga Lake. We had seven bears visit our home in the course of about six weeks. This prompted the removal of bird feeders and the addition of large, lockable wooden doors on the woodshed to protect our garbage cans and chicken feed.

I often encourage my students to consider ingesting behaviors by asking, "How do you think this animal makes a living?" In other words, given its physical characteristics, how does an animal hunt for or secure food? Looking at skulls—eye placement, beak or tooth structure, and nasal cavities—can reveal much about an animal's foraging habits. There is a saying I often share that helps my students remember how to determine predator versus prey species: "Eyes on the side, likes to hide; eyes in front, likes to hunt." This little saying is often true, but many, if not most, predators can also become prey to something larger. Think of a snake, for instance. Snakes hunt a range of prey, including earthworms, frogs, and even deer, but they are also regularly eaten by an array of predators. On a recent trip to Maryland, I observed a chipmunk eating what appeared to be a ring-necked snake.

Questions to ask about ingesting behaviors:

· What does this animal eat?
· How is it equipped to secure its food, and where is this food found?
· Does the animal store food? If so, where?
· Does the design of its feet or talons give a clue as to how this animal lives or hunts?

Black bear sign is regularly spotted in the smooth bark of aspen trees. (iStock/Natalie Ruffing)

ELIMINATION

I have often been able to locate bats in my barn, attics, and other nearby locations by looking for bat droppings on the ground or floor. It can be fun to bring young trackers to these spots and ask what it is they think they are seeing. Students often guess that a mouse is the culprit, but the fact that the similar-looking scat is found concentrated in the middle of the floor or in one spot suggests something else. It can take some time, but eventually someone looks up to discover a bat house or a space in the rafters that provides a sanctuary. Sadly, such indicators have become far less common as eastern bat populations have succumbed to the deadly fungal infection white nose syndrome.

Leaving scat and/or marking with urine can also be a way for animals to communicate a variety of information to each other. This realm of animal behavior has great potential for in-depth study. An old friend told me she had discovered that a bobcat had visited the back of her property where she had dumped her cat box. To me this interesting situation leads to more questions than answers, such as: Does domestic cat urine smell enough like wild cat urine to have tricked the bobcat? What kind of information did the bobcat gain from the visit? Did the bobcat return the message with some kind of marking?

Questions to ask about elimination behaviors:

- Does the animal in question void or defecate in a specific place?
- Does it mark with its urine or scat?
- Does its urine have a specific odor?
- What does its scat look like?
- Does it hide or bury its scat?
- Does the animal eat its own feces?
- How does its scat vary in consistency over the year as the result of changes in diet?

SELF-MAINTENANCE

Keeping clean and well groomed, as well as striving for an ideal state of homeostasis, is an essential part of most animals' lives. Contrary to some common—and ignorant—assumptions, most wild animals are quite clean and spend a good deal of time engaging in self-maintenance. Well-kept feathers and fur do their job better and indicate healthy wildlife. After spending enough hours in the field, you will probably routinely witness this baseline behavior. I can't think of a bird or mammal species I've observed that I haven't seen cleaning or grooming itself at one time or another.

One young beaver, who my family nicknamed Merle, made a den in our backyard pond and was a regular and meticulous groomer. One observation I made was that he groomed much more often and more thoroughly when the water was cold. This seemed to imply that a well-kept coat helped to keep him warm.

Questions to consider when noting self-maintenance behaviors for a specific animal:

· How does the animal groom or take care of itself?
· Does it have special glands it uses to oil its fur or feathers?
· Does it engage in specific behaviors to help remove parasites?

RESTING

Resting relates to the rule of energy conservation. Once all of a creature's immediate needs are met, the thing to do is rest. This behavior is exhibited regularly and in a multitude of ways. Birds perch, deer bed, and turtles bask.

Resting is generally an excellent indicator of baseline behavior. As one of the most common and easily observable behaviors you will encounter, it usually means that for the moment the animal is content and senses no nearby predators. One exception that every observer should know: resting due to illness or injury. On many occasions I have come across animals that are compromised in some way and are bedded down because they are healing, sick, or dying.

As the years have passed and my skills have progressed, I have encountered more and more resting predators (usually foxes). Discovering resting wild animals, especially predators, is always an indication that you are doing a good job of staying invisible.

Questions to ask about resting behaviors for a specific animal:

- Does this animal have a particular time of day and/or place that it rests?
- Does the animal rest alone or as part of a group?
- Is the animal's health compromised in any way?

INCLEMENT WEATHER STRATEGIES

Dealing with cold, precipitation, and weather events is something all animals have to contend with. It's important to learn to recognize behaviors that seem to be associated with changes in season or notable weather events. I often notice an increase in deer activity before winter storms. They seem to know when the weather is going to take a turn for the worse and do their best to prepare.

Questions to ask about inclement weather strategies for a specific animal:

- How does the animal cope with winter?
- Does it escape the oncoming cold by migrating? If so, how does it migrate and where does it go?
- Does the animal hibernate or retreat to a state of dormancy?
- If the animal hibernates, how and when does it reemerge?
- Does it store food and/or accumulate fat to ensure its survival?

MOLTING OR SHEDDING

Molting (of feathers, shells, or antlers) or shedding (of fur or skin) is a component of the annual cycle for a great number of wild animals. While this is a fairly benign process for some, for others molting or shedding places them in a state of vulnerability. (More on this in Chapter 5.)

Insects molt by discarding their exoskeletons. Evidence of this process is most visible in my area during the emergence of brood cicadas, when their ghostly casings can be found in trees up and down the East Coast. Depending on the species, every thirteen or seventeen

Resting—or more specifically in the case of these turtles, basking—is a common way for reptiles of all kinds to get warm. (iStock/J. Michael Jones)

The eyes of this garter snake have clouded over, indicating that it is in the process of getting ready to shed its skin.

years the Finger Lakes region plays host to a mass surfacing of these large invertebrates.

All reptiles shed their skins, but snakes discard their skins in one piece. They do not have separate eyelids, and the special scales or "caps" that cover their eyes are part of their skin and must be discarded as the animal grows. During the shedding process, which can take three or four days, the outer dermis takes on a milky, ashen pallor and occludes the snake's vision. A snake's mobility during shedding is impaired in great part by its inability to see. By contrast, lizards have eyelids and shed their skin in sections.

Adult Canada geese molt once each year during the summer as a component of their annual self-maintenance. The old feathers are replaced with new. During this time, these geese, as well as their recently hatched offspring, are unable to fly. They stay close to the water during this period in an effort to avoid land predation.

Questions to consider here:

· If evidence of shedding is found, to what kind of animal does this skin, feather, hair, or antler belong?

- Does shedding or molting compromise the safety or senses of the animal?

Reproductive Behaviors

Reproductive behaviors revolve around the big goal of creating offspring to ensure the continuation of the species. The drive to reproduce and ensure survival often trumps all other concerns. There are many behaviors, in fact, that are *part of* the reproductive cycle: securing territory, establishing hierarchy, fighting for the right to mate, posturing, posting scents, performing courtship rituals, signaling receptivity, and engaging in pre-rut activity. The ones we will explore here are courtship, pair bonding, territorial behaviors, and nurturing behaviors.

Changes in body shape, calls, or coloration (displays) are also related to reproduction. Reproductive behaviors can mark at least one point in an animal's yearly cycle when it is more vulnerable. (Find more on this perspective in Chapter 5.) If you suspect that a behavior has something to do with reproduction in some way, ask why and be open to possibilities.

COURTSHIP

Courtship can encompass any number of behaviors that ultimately are part of the mating game. Some indications of courtship may be difficult to detect, such as odors and subtle visual cues. Others may be relatively easy to observe. Where I live, the strutting of male turkeys in the springtime is an obvious courtship behavior, where the tom is attempting to impress and attract females. I regularly see similar strutting behavior in urban birds such as pigeons and house finches. These kinds of pre-mating behaviors often go hand in hand with male-to-male aggression.

Questions to ask when noting courtship behaviors of a specific animal:

- Does the animal you are observing show and/or use new plumage or change color?

- How do the male and female display a willingness to mate?
- How might the suitability of a mate be observed? (Females as well as males may be looking for a mate that is up to the requirements of raising young—strong, healthy and capable.)

PAIR BONDING

At the risk of anthropomorphizing, I generally see the rituals and behaviors that go along with pair bonding as sweet and touching. These are behaviors (not seen in all species) that help to reinforce the bonds between mated pairs, between offspring, and sometimes between group members. The cardinal pair that frequents my bird-feeder can be observed in the spring with the male feeding the female. This could be viewed as a courtship behavior or as a bonding behavior that reinforces the tie they have to each other, since cardinals typically mate for life. Sometimes the distinction isn't clear.

Questions to ask about pair bonding behaviors:

- How does this particular species enact its pair bonding ritual or rituals?
- When are these behaviors generally seen?
- Is the bond created a seasonal one or is it lifelong?

TERRITORIAL BEHAVIORS

A good territory provides shelter, water, food, and cover and ensures enough resources to raise young. Territories vary greatly in size and features, depending on the animal in question. But we can generalize by saying it is important and worth an animal's effort to establish and defend its territory. Territorial behaviors can include sound or singing; posturing, heckling, or fighting with an intruder; and fleeing from a predator, in which case things have gone very wrong and an adult has had to abandon its nest or den as the young have been preyed upon.

One morning I was awakened from a deep sleep after spending the night in a lean-to near the shores of Fairview Lake in New Jersey, to find two male turkeys engaged in a territorial dispute. I have observed a number of animal clashes over the years, but nothing I had ever seen

All birds need to secure a territory that ensures enough space and resources for food procurement and nesting opportunities. Territorial disputes, such as this one between Galapagos mockingbirds, are a common behavior that is mostly seen between members of the same species. (Melissa Groo)

compared with these warring toms. They were out for blood. They wrapped necks, bit, clawed, and charged one other, occasionally bursting into the air. This battle went on for more than forty-five minutes. Such is the instinctual drive to establish territorial and mating rights in the animal kingdom.

Questions you can ask about territorial behaviors:

· How does the animal mark its territory?
· How are territories established? Do territories overlap?
· At what age does the animal seek out its own territory?

NURTURING BEHAVIORS

It can be argued that the primary job of any animal is to ensure the future of its species. Nurturing and bringing up young is a significant element of this task.

At my home we have strategically mounted a bluebird house on our garden gate that we can see from our kitchen window. This has made for wonderfully easy viewing. Our local bluebirds have been using this house for many years, at times producing as many as three broods per season. It is immensely satisfying to watch the parents bring food to the young who are still bound to the house. The offerings brought range in size from small insects and moths to caterpillars that seem comically too large for a baby bird.

Questions to consider about nurturing behaviors for a specific animal:

- How are the young provided and cared for? How are they fed and taught to feed themselves? Do parents groom and otherwise maintain the health and well-being of their young?
- At what age are the young encouraged to strike out on their own?
- Should the need arise, how do parents defend the den or nest site?

Social Behaviors

Social behaviors are an array of interactions that happen between two or more animals usually of the same species. They involve communication, socializing, symbiosis, antagonism, defense, alarm, grief, and nervousness (bluffing and bluster).

COMMUNICATION

Animals communicate through a variety of means. Crows, for example, use an array of complex language. As the PBS documentary *A Murder of Crows* illustrates, these scavengers are highly intelligent and have the capacity to relay the presence of an impending threat to other members of the group—and even recognize human faces.

In the interest of health and safety, animals often express themselves in nonconfrontational ways. For instance, simple posturing by a

This pair of male turkeys are likely in competition with each other as they display and try to attract females to breed with. Sometimes males will fight with each other as they vie for dominance in battles that can be very intense. (iStock/BackyardProduction)

dominant male can communicate to subordinate males who the boss is with no actual fight taking place.

Questions to ask about communication behaviors:

· What sounds does the animal make and what do these sounds mean?
· Are there specific body postures that communicate explicit information?
· Are there specific times of the year when these behaviors occur?
· Does the animal use scent and/or visual cues to communicate?

SOCIALIZING

Many animals, including birds, are social. Being part of a social group can confer the benefit of safety in numbers. Aspects of social behavior may include establishment of a hierarchy, as well as an array of interesting vocalizations and behaviors such as grooming, communal nesting, and co-parenting.

Turkeys are an excellent example of a species that is very social. Outside of the nesting season, most turkeys are found in groups. They use a variety of calls to communicate with each other. Turkeys also have excellent vision and are ever vigilant. Late one winter a flock of hens came through my lower field. As they fed on sensitive ferns near the pond, they appeared to be a bit nervous and seemed to literally be looking over their shoulders. From my front window I kept watch. Several minutes later the cause for their unease appeared. A lone coyote made his way down the hill toward the field and the birds. With a dozen or so sets of watchful eyes trained on him, however, the predator seemed to know he had little chance of getting close enough for a kill.

Questions to consider about socializing behaviors for a specific animal:

· Is the animal solitary or is it part of a socialized group?
· Is there a hierarchy, and if so, how is it established?
· Do animals in a group bond with one other? If so, how is this expressed?
· Are there any cooperative behaviors?
· What kind of vocalizations have you heard?

SYMBIOTIC BEHAVIORS

When two species have a close relationship with one another, it is referred to as symbiosis. Usually, but not always, this relationship benefits everyone involved. There are several categories of symbiosis. *Commensalism* is a relationship where one species benefits and the other is unharmed but gains little or nothing. An example of this would be when a mature burdock seed attaches to an animal's fur and is dispersed with no harm or benefit to the host. *Parasitism* happens when one species benefits at the expense of the other. Think fleas, mosquitoes, and any number of other familiar creatures. *Endosymbiosis* is defined as one being living inside another. This tends to be seen on a micro level. *Mutualism* is the version of symbiosis thought of most often, in which both species benefit from the relationship.

In my neck of the woods it is not uncommon to see deer and turkeys hanging out with each other. This is a mutually beneficial relationship in which everyone is safer. The deer have excellent hearing; the turkeys have superior eyesight. Together they make for an incredibly aware group.

Questions about symbiotic behaviors for a specific animal:

· What kind of symbiosis am I witnessing?
· Are species in proximity to each other benefiting in some way? (The idea of safety in numbers is true within a group of the same species as well as within a mixed group. On countless occasions, the alarms of a single individual alert the masses to an incoming predator.)

ANTAGONISTIC BEHAVIORS

Antagonistic behaviors are similar to alarms (discussed more in Chapter 7) in that both are dramatic. Pay attention to the details, though—antagonistic behaviors are often seen within the same species during hierarchical, food-related disputes, territorial battles, and mating rites, and are not always the result of a predatory threat. Antagonistic behaviors tend to relate to dominance and are really about backing an opponent down and into submission. Although antagonistic behavior can express itself through nonphysical posturing, this category can also get very physical and has the potential to lead to injury and death.

Once, while running along a ridge on the Finger Lakes Trail in upstate New York, I came to an abrupt stop. A red fox lay dead on the path. This animal had a thick, healthy coat and, save for the gashes around its neck, appeared pristine and unmolested. Canines generally don't get along. Despite all being in the dog family, wolves kill coyotes, and coyotes kill foxes. The dead animal lying in front of me was likely a victim of this familial discord. I am fascinated by this potential area of study and see that there is much to learn in this realm.

Questions to consider about antagonistic behaviors:

- Does the animal show signs of aggression toward members of its own species and/or other species?
- When and how do these behaviors manifest?
- Can this animal inflict harm on a potential adversary?
- What reason or reasons seem to motivate conflicts?

DEFENSIVE BEHAVIORS

Defensive behaviors fall into the category of alarms and should alert the observer to a nonbaseline event. These behaviors, which can include evasive maneuvers, posturing, and physical conflict, are in general dramatic and at the very least should point your attention toward a predator.

Many years ago while walking up a dirt road in New Jersey, I encountered an eastern hognose snake. My companion, a schoolteacher, gently prodded it with a stick. This prompted the snake, who felt more than threatened, to barf up a frog, roll onto its belly, and play dead. This stunt was easily exposed, as each time the teacher flipped the snake right side up, it would immediately flip itself back over and feign death.

A defensive behavior that I see much more regularly is the broken wing display enacted by killdeer. A parent killdeer pretending to be injured draws potential predators away from the nest site or young. This is one of many behaviors that can be interpreted in multiple ways, in this case as nurturing or defensive behavior.

Questions you can ask about defensive behaviors:

- How does the animal defend itself when threatened?
- What postures does it assume?
- Does the animal use specific strategies to present a more menacing or unattractive appearance?
- If the situation escalates, is the prey species able to defend itself? If so, what tools does it have at its disposal?

ALARM

Recognizing the alarms of animals when they feel vulnerable or threatened is a dynamic and powerful experience. Familiarity with the social behaviors already mentioned will have a profound impact on your

I discovered this killdeer in the gravel alongside a set of railroad tracks. I had unknowingly gotten too close to its nest and the bird was attempting to draw me away by pretending to have a broken wing. I immediately became extra careful to ensure that I didn't step on the camouflaged eggs as I moved away.

awareness of this particular behavior. It may surprise you, in fact, how frequently cries of alarm are uttered not only in wilderness settings but also in urban environments.

Almost daily I notice some form of alarm caused by the presence or pursuits of a predator. One of the most common forms of alarm I experience is the mobbing behavior of crows aimed toward red-tailed hawks. Then there were the alarms provoked by our old cat, Luna, who was unfortunately a very effective hunter. If she was outside and I wasn't sure where she was, all I had to do was listen for the angry calls of our backyard birds. Usually it was the wrens that would announce her location. I would walk toward the disturbance and call to her, and almost without exception she would come meowing toward me from her hiding place in the thicket.

The intensity of the alarm is almost always in direct proportion to the severity of the threat. A lackadaisical housecat lounging on a suburban porch may elicit little more than mild disapproval from neighboring songbirds, whereas a Cooper's hawk will throw these same birds into an eruption of protective maneuvers. I once observed what seemed to be odd and dangerous behavior from a house sparrow that dove under my slow-moving car as I pulled into my office parking lot, only to discover that a Cooper's hawk was afoot, hunting the hedges and trees of the urban wilderness.

By contrast, bald eagles, despite being apex raptors, prompt little concern from songbirds. I have on more than one occasion seen blackbirds preening not ten feet from a perched eagle. These large birds of prey are simply not built to pursue small, maneuverable game and won't waste their energy trying. (I often wonder if small birds purposely use eagles as bodyguards of a sort, hedging their bets that smaller, bird-hunting hawks such as sharp-shinned won't come too close to a larger predator's space.) Geese, on the other hand, are a common enough prey for bald eagles that they may react strongly when one is present. Again, the severity of the alarm corresponds to the abilities of the threat. Be mindful, too, that the absence of an alarm does not necessarily indicate an absence of predators. At times I have chanced upon sleeping or resting foxes whose presence was not broadcast by the local alarm system. There are a number of plausible explanations for this lack of commotion, including:

· There are no birds in the immediate vicinity.
· Birds are present, but instead of wasting their time with a resting animal, they're maintaining a watchful eye as they go about their business.
· The predator has simply eluded detection by its prey.
· The predator has completed a successful ambush and is feasting (or has already feasted) on prey. Any immediate threat has subsided.
· Prey species may give space/berth around a predator's den or nest.

When a true alarm is taking place, everyone that is potentially affected reacts. Animals have an investment in paying attention to the vocalizations, reactions, and body language of everyone around them. No animal is an island unto itself; it must constantly adapt to emergent needs. Baseline behaviors generally stop, and everyone in proximity pays attention, takes safety measures, and remains vigilant. What's going on and why? remains a potent question in this regard.

One pivotal question related to alarming is: How does the animal posture, respond, and vocalize in the face of perceived threats?

GRIEF

Animals with highly developed nervous systems can and do grieve the loss of a loved one. I have witnessed this behavior in birds, once observing the distress of a mother robin whose young had been killed by a housecat. Her alarms went on for hours. Grieving has been observed in other species as well, including dolphins, primates, and companion animals. (For more about this, see *How Animals Grieve* by Barbara J. King.)

Questions to ask if you suspect an animal is grieving:

- How is the animal expressing itself?
- What is the cause of its grief?
- Do animals hold on to trauma over time?
- Do animals who are less social have the same capacity for grief as more social creatures?

NERVOUSNESS—BLUFFING AND BLUSTER

An animal can demonstrate discomfort with a situation in several ways. A deer, for example, may take a few cautious steps toward a perceived threat, stomp her feet, and snort. She may also put her head down for a moment, pretending to graze, then suddenly look up in an attempt to catch the perceived threat. This behavior serves a dual purpose. The stomp or snort can startle the threat into moving, as well as alert other animals in the vicinity. The alarm behavior can be unique to the individual species. Beaver react by slapping their tails on the water. Woodchucks respond with a sharp whistle, and birds vocalize a distress alarm.

One evening while I was writing this book, my home was visited by a hungry black bear. From the safety of our bay window, we observed the bear, who had been drawn to the bird feeder fifteen feet from our house. This animal was incredibly vocal, making an array of sounds such as moaning, blowing, chomping, and huffing. In the moment, this behavior seemed overly aggressive. The next day, after some internet research, I found some enlightening information on the North American Bear Center website. All of the sounds and behaviors displayed by this bear fell into the category of harmless bluster caused by a state of nervousness. This made complete sense once I viewed footage from my trailcam, which showed that our visitor was a mama bear! She had sent three cubs into the upper branches of the tree hosting the bird feeder, all of whom descended later that night.

Questions to consider about nervous behavior by a specific animal:

· Is the animal posturing in a way that indicates nervousness?
· Has it bluffed or made sounds that show it is concerned?
· Has it lifted its head up so as to hear, see, or smell better?

Birds: A Case Study in Animal Language and Behavior

Birds provide an excellent window into in animal language and behavior, whether in wild, rural, or more urbanized settings. In *What the Robin Knows: How Birds Reveal the Secrets of the Natural World*, author Jon Young details the impact that an understanding of bird language and behavior can have on your awareness. My introduction to Young's work came many years ago when I participated in a daylong workshop at the Rune Hill Earth Awareness School in Spencer, New York.

Young teaches that by asking basic questions about what you're hearing and seeing, you will become more proficient at determining what kind of life-supporting behaviors you've observed (or, if there is a threat, what predator is the cause of the alarm). An understanding of fundamental bird language helps us frame the question, What's going on here, and why? It helps train the eyes and ears to identify certain patterns of behavior.

Young establishes a foundation for understanding bird language by encouraging the reader to focus on vocalizations in conjunction

It took almost a week for me to figure out the mystery of an alarming robin during a family visit to Cape Cod. The cause of some alarms will become obvious with time, while many may remain a mystery for a lifetime. (iStock/donyanedomam)

with body language and what he calls the five voices. The first four are song, male-to-male aggression, adolescent begging, and companion calls. (I categorize these as life-supporting behaviors.) The fifth type is alarming. As we have already learned, alarming implies concern and reveals a possible predatory event is under way. In *What the Robin Knows*, Young urges readers to pay attention to the positioning and movements of birds as they react to perceived threats. Positioning in conjunction with alarming helps determine what (often unseen) threat is moving in the environment.

In the summer of 2015, I spent a week on Cape Cod, where my parents had rented a house in celebration of their fiftieth wedding anniversary. The residence was set on a beautiful property, the back lawn sloping down toward a pond bustling with the activity of amphibians and small fish. This particular house was nestled in a historic neighborhood marked by unkempt hedges, old trees, and wetlands. Although we were in civilization, the neighborhood had a decidedly feral appeal.

On our first day there, I tuned in to the incessant alarming of a robin. I made my way across the porch, hoping to interpret her call. As I drew closer, I was unable to see anything that would elicit such a response. The thick underbrush and hedges between properties made it difficult to see. I crept onto the lawn and made my way along the edge of the property but was still completely uncertain. Over the course of the week I heard this robin several more times, but I was unable to determine the cause of her distress. I began to wonder if this event would remain a mystery.

During our final day at the Cape, I once again heard the robin's call—this time from a large tree in the front yard. The house where we were staying was built around a windmill that was once used to draw groundwater to feed the property, and from inside the house I made my way to the top of the windmill's spiral staircase. Through a large open window I found myself exchanging glances with the robin that had eluded me all week. She had a mouthful of insects and continued to alarm with hardly a break. Why, I wondered, did she have a beak full of insects? And why was she alarming? Then it all suddenly made sense.

The robin was pointing to the answer. In a towering spruce, perched at the same height, was a red-tailed hawk. After about thirty minutes, the hawk flew away. The robin ceased alarming and fluttered into a nearby thicket.

If you aren't sure whether what you are seeing and/or hearing from birds is an alarm, ask these questions:

· Are multiple birds or bird species involved?
· Are the calls sharp, loud, and intense, or have the birds gone quieter?
· Are you seeing mobbing, where multiple birds act in concert in an attempt to bring attention to and/or drive off a predator?
· Are birds making a specific alarm in a specific way toward a specific predator?

Brian Mertins has an excellent article on bird alarms, complete with video clips, at his Nature Mentoring website (nature-mentor.com).

Exercises

- Choose an animal native to your area (and one that is highly visible) to be the focus of an ethogram study. (Songbirds, chipmunks, and squirrels are excellent candidates.) Observe a number of these animals at various times of the day for a period of two weeks. Do you notice any specific behaviors that emerge as characteristic? Any that appear to be atypical? For those behaviors exhibited with the greatest frequency, did you see a clear indication of why they were performed?

- Take a walk in the woods and note how the animals in your environment respond to your presence. Whereas arboreal rodents like chickarees may chatter and disperse, what do you experience with larger animals such as deer? If you cross paths with a turtle, does it retreat to the comfort of nearby waters or hole up in its shell? To what extent does the proximity of your person play into these decisions, and how do these decisions correspond to the rule of energy conservation?

- In the concluding anecdote about my visit to Cape Cod, I was able to determine that the robin was alarming because of the presence of a red-tailed hawk. Although I successfully solved the mystery of what was prompting the alarming, other questions were left unanswered. See if you can solve these riddles: Why did the robin have a beak full of insects? Was the robin worried that the hawk would attempt an ambush? Did the thicket play a role in this scenario?

CHAPTER 5

Animal Vulnerabilities

"The history of life on earth has been a
history of interaction between living things
and their surroundings."

—RACHEL CARSON, *SILENT SPRING*

t's early spring, and the icy waters have begun to thaw. Snowmelt fills the modest creek I am approaching. Here, driven by instinct and warming waters, my quarry journeys from the safety of a massive lake to spawn. The need to reproduce overtakes prudence as hundreds of fish struggle upstream. Without rod and reel, spear or bow, I stalk the prolific redhorse sucker with nothing more than my bare hands.

There's a rhythm to the water's ebb and flow, and the fish disrupt these patterns as they swim upstream. I reach a small set of rapids where they've congregated in the shallows off the main channel. I move so slowly that I become part of the landscape.

As I cautiously wade into the creek, several fish fight their way through the current. One slips behind a rock to seek refuge from the current. I can't see her, but I'm certain of her presence. The disturbances created by the moving water provide me with a bit of cover. After a deliberate and slow approach, I crouch when I am in range, steadying my weight with one hand against the floor of the creek bed. My free hand glides with smooth precision into the water.

I gently touch the tail of the fish, and my hand slides along her body as she undulates gently back and forth. With my thumb on one side and my fingers on the other, I inch along the fish's spine toward her head. I am always amazed at how if a person moves slowly enough, he can be in contact with a fish without alarm or awareness. If I grab her anywhere but the gill slit, the layer of mucus that coats her scales will allow her to slip from my grasp. Moments later I clutch the fish and press her into the bottom of the creek and then remove my three-pound catch from the frigid, rushing waters. This fish becomes a meal.

Annual Cycles

Everything in the natural world is connected to recurring cycles, whether it's a sunrise, a season, or the weather. Breeding and raising young, resolving territorial disputes, and evading predation are but a few of the demands that an animal faces during its annual cycle.

All predators take advantage of, and profit from, yearly vulnerabilities. For many animals at the top of the food chain, survival often hinges on the ability to exploit these cycles. Raptors snatch fledgling songbirds from their nests. Bears capitalize on the spring salmon run. Raccoons desecrate the unguarded nests of snapping turtles. Throughout recorded history, humans across the globe have also turned to these moments of vulnerability to feed their family and community.

As a student and teacher of nature-oriented skills, I view each animal I encounter through the lens of vulnerability. I ask myself when in its life cycle it is most likely to be caught off guard, exposed, tied to one

---

PREVIOUS IMAGE This common loon, which was nested on a small Island on Long Lake in New York, was attempting to make itself less conspicuous by literally laying low in an effort to avoid drawing attention to its nest as a canoe paddled past.

Thoughtful Engagement during Vulnerable Times

Several of the "Guidelines for Thoughtful Engagement" in Chapter 1 touch on respecting animal vulnerabilities. To review:

- Avoid causing unnecessary disturbance or stress to wildlife.
- Remain sensitive to seasonal pressures. Certain times of the year and situations can be especially trying for animals.
- Be extra considerate around animals that are raising young.
- Be considerate of the time of year if you choose to call. In winter, some birds, for example, may have a limited food supply and may be operating with a very small energy reserve.

This chapter goes into more detail about the times of year and situations that can be challenging for animals so you can be extra considerate at these times and in these situations.

particular spot, or otherwise left susceptible to predation. Knowing the different types of annual cycles has aided me, both for hunting or simply for observation and study.

Annual cycles manifest in forms as varied as the world's inhabitants. Here I examine some of the most common seasonal rituals. Looking at the life of an animal through the lens of vulnerability is a shift in perspective on many of the behaviors introduced in Chapter 4.

Migration

If an animal migrates, this is arguably the greatest point of vulnerability in its yearly cycle. Many birds, for example, have wintering grounds and breeding grounds but are far less familiar with all the places in between. Even though they may use the same fields and wetlands as resting spots during their journeys, they spend less time in these places and therefore have no way of knowing the potential threats that await. Driving

Snow geese can often be seen in vast flocks during migration to and from their breeding grounds in the high Arctic. (iStock/Spondylolithesis)

outside the fringes of the Montezuma National Wildlife Refuge near Seneca Falls, New York, one autumn, I was startled by gunfire echoing from a nearby field. I turned to see several Canada geese falling from the sky. These birds, drawn to a privately owned field that offered a presumably safe asylum, were unaware of the dangers lurking below.

Migrating to and from wintering grounds and back to summer homes is energy intensive and not without its vulnerabilities, but in the long run it is an effective strategy for overall survival and reproduction. Being able to continue to eat in warm locations has obvious benefits. But we might ask, Why not just stay south? The answer is about pressure and resources. By returning north, migrating birds have comparatively less pressure as well as more resources when they need them the most—namely, when nesting and rearing young.

Besides the uncertainty and more obvious risks that come with migration, such as predation and injury, there are also manmade threats that kill huge numbers of birds each year. These threats include wind turbines, glass buildings, and power lines. Global climate change may also be increasing the challenges associated with this undertaking. Examples of new or increased hazards during migration can include severe weather events and missed opportunities when migrating birds' timing doesn't correspond with ripened fruit or insect hatches.

Mating and Spawning

The drive to reproduce takes precedence over all other concerns; an animal's primary reason for being is to ensure survival of its species. This imperative can turn otherwise cautious individuals into lovesick drones preoccupied only with courtship. I have observed such behavior exhibited by animals including deer, fish, woodchucks, and snakes as males seek out a receptive mate. I once saw a large female garter snake glide across my lawn. Ten minutes later, several smaller males followed her scent. I stood with my feet just off their path as they slithered by.

Creatures that spawn (such as fish, amphibians, and crustaceans) are governed by the same impulses as other animals (mammals, birds, reptiles, insects, and mollusks), and spawning is greatly influenced by changing water temperatures in conjunction with the seasons. Mole salamanders, for example, often emerge en masse during the spring thaw, which prompts them to migrate and breed. In late March or early April, increasing temperatures and heavy rains cue these large amphibians to emerge from their burrows and make the daring trek to nearby vernal pools. These transient ponds, created in depressions from a combination of snowmelt and rainwater, dry up by midsummer and are therefore not capable of sustaining larger, predatory species such as fish.

My friend Don still lives in suburban Buffalo where he and I grew up. He continues to fish the tributaries feeding into Lake Ontario. Don is so well versed in the spawning habits of northern pike that he can predict their migration patterns based solely on water temperature. One day I followed him as we explored a creek that runs near our old neighborhood. Don identified a comfortable access point and dipped a thermometer into the current to determine the water's temperature. He deemed it just right. After a quick search, Don spotted a modest-sized pike, confirmation that the fish could be counted on to follow their age-old rhythm.

Nesting and Denning

The act of nesting, creating a den, or otherwise finding a place to raise young is not without risk—being tied to one place is in itself a dangerous proposition. Once it is discovered, a home may become a buffet counter for a capable predator. A nest of rabbit kits makes a fine meal for an enterprising fox, and other young mammals frolicking in or around a den site can easily be targeted by birds of prey.

As a child I remember discovering all manner of defenseless offspring. It was clear to me that all young are susceptible to predation, from nests of duck eggs to cached white-tailed fawns to broods of eastern cottontails.

One spring afternoon while leading a youth group on an orientation exercise, I came across a den beneath an old root ball. Looking inside, my eyes quickly adjusted to find six canine pups. I instructed my students to take a closer look. Knowing that we had likely startled the parents, we quickly departed. The next day a friend sought out this same den and found it uninhabited. To these feral dogs, this encounter was far too worrisome to risk staying.

Bearing, Feeding, and Raising Young

Young animals are vulnerable to a multitude of threats. Most have to be fed and are tied to the place where they were born. (Exceptions to this are species that do not care for their young, including most fish, reptiles, and amphibians.) Parents must leave the nest or den to forage or hunt, leaving eggs or young open to predation. Many animals learn invaluable survival skills from their parents, but some young are self-absorbed, aloof, and uninformed in the ways of the world. Parents, despite their best efforts to pass along their wisdom, do not always succeed.

One spring I found that a large woodchuck had slipped through my family's garden fence and raided our lettuce bed. Using a live trap, I captured and released her several miles away in a tract of state forest. Several days later I discovered that this particular woodchuck was, in fact, a mother. I watched as five kits emerged from the brush to graze on our lawn. Because these young were too light to trigger my live trap,

Signs of Dens, Nests, and Cavity Homes

An alarm reaction from adults may indicate that you have accidentally gotten close to an animal's den, nest, or cavity. Here are other signs to look for:

- fresh dirt, rocks, or wood chips excavated from the den or cavity
- trampled vegetation or moss
- building materials or gathered vegetation
- food remnants
- scat, or white streaking in the case of birds
- nearby hair, feathers, or bones
- young in den area or nest site

I sat nearby and pulled on a cord from a hidden vantage to trip the doors.

I soon realized how inexperienced and vulnerable young animals can be. As I walked across the lawn to check my Havahart, I spotted one kit feeding by the garden fence. With quick and deliberate movements (quicker, at least, than a proper stalk), I lowered myself to the ground and made my way toward him. I captured the woodchuck with my bare hands and placed him, along with his siblings, in a large wooden box in my mudroom. I caught the remaining two in a similar fashion and released them in the same area as their mother.

This is a cautionary tale, as I have since learned that relocating wildlife is problematic. Not only is it hard on the wildlife because they are not familiar with their new area, making them more vulnerable, but it is also illegal in New York. The proper thing to do is to contact Animal Control wherever you live if you find unwanted wildlife in your yard, and let a professional handle the situation.

Pine martens are skilled hunters found in mixed conifer and boreal forests in Canada, Alaska, and parts of the northern United States. (iStock/KeithSzafranski)

Molting or Shedding

Molting or shedding increases animals' vulnerability as well. When a snake molts, for example, its skin begins to loosen, the area over its eyes becomes cloudy, and its vision is compromised until the old skin is removed. (As explained in the previous chapter, snakes' skin covers their whole body, including their eyes.) Molting snakes tend to be more cautious and reactionary. I choose to leave our resident garter snakes alone as they go through the process of shedding.

For crayfish and similar creatures, shedding can be a safety issue. When the old, hard exoskeleton is shed, a new soft skin is revealed. Until this hardens, the animal is at greater risk of predation. Hermit crabs also shed their housing as they mature. These saltwater crustaceans differ greatly from organisms like terrapins and mollusks in that they are not joined to their shells. Instead, hermit crabs take up residence in vacant shells for protection but are extremely vulnerable to predation when moving from one shell to another.

After this unfortunate bobcat was hit by a car, a witness covered it with a piece of canvas and gently moved it from the road to a nearby lawn. When it was uncovered the cat paused for a moment, stood up, and took off into a nearby thicket. No sign of it was found the next day. This is an example of an acceptable intervention with an injured animal.

Sickness, Injury, and Old Age

Biological factors that make animals vulnerable by compromising or degrading their abilities include sickness, injury, and old age. Sick, injured, or dying animals are quickly culled from the flow of life. Such cherry picking is a sensible choice for most predators, promising a greater chance of return on any energy that's expended. It also strengthens a herd, flock, or colony by removing its weakest members.

While canoeing one winter around Howland Island in central New York, I observed several immature bald eagles attempting to pluck an injured mallard from the water. With each attempt, the duck—which for some reason was unable to fly—submerged and disappeared. Sometimes the eagles circled for several moments over the water, but at other times they preferred to alight on a nearby tree while a companion took his or her turn. For half an hour I watched this drama unfold. By the time I paddled away, the eagles still hadn't succeeded.

Unless you have confidently deemed the situation safe and are able to help (for example, aiding an injured bird), it is best to be extra vigilant and distant from animals that are compromised in some way resulting from trauma or illness. Besides not wanting to stress the animal, you might face the possibility of getting rabies or some other concerning disease or getting bitten or scratched.

How do you identify an injured or sick animal? Both observable behavior and the actions of other animals can give clues.

Clues from Observable Behavior

When an animal becomes injured or sick, it may exhibit any number or combination of behaviors that are not typically seen. Behaviors and visual clues to look for:

- open mouth, which can indicate breathing issues or possibly a head injury
- heavy, labored breathing
- obvious injury such as a broken bone protruding through the skin
- bleeding from the mouth, nose, or ears
- staggering or drunken movement
- odd posture

Clues from the Actions of Other Animals

Injured, dead, or dying animals become the focus of attention of an array of wildlife. Even smaller predators will keep an eye on larger predators' efforts in taking down a sick or injured animal in hopes of getting a meal. Things to observe in this realm:

- vultures converging on a kill
- convergence of predators around a dead or injured bird or animal, which can lead to a trickling down of alarm calls from birds and smaller animals
- an increase in concentration of predatory as well as scavenger tracks in an area
- blood, fur, and bones scattered but concentrated in an area
- a predator patiently following an injured animal, waiting for death or the right opportunity to bring the prey down

If You See a Young Animal Alone

I always err on the side of not interfering with a young animal that appears to be alone. In most cases the animal is likely fine and the parent isn't far away. It may be worth observing the animal from afar to be sure. Signs that a young animal may truly be alone include these:

○ The animal is covered in ticks or fleas.
○ The animal follows you around.
○ You see some sign that the mother has been killed or wounded.
○ The animal is weak and/or dehydrated.
○ A significant amount of time has passed and no parent has come to visit the young one.

Environmental Factors

The final category of vulnerability concerns those constraints imposed on wildlife by the environment; factors that are far less predictable than the other vulnerabilities. Weather events in particular can impact food and water availability. These circumstances are not necessarily present each year but can have a profound influence on an ecosystem's inhabitants. Dynamics including drought, flooding, wildfires, weather, and temperature extremes can significantly affect wildlife.

Drought

All life depends on water to survive. Unless there is an unwanted surplus, water means life, and drought conditions place a significant strain on the natural world.

Drought often prompts animals to congregate near water holes or on floodplains, where plant life is abundant. While I was writing this book, portions of upstate New York experienced what the US Drought Monitor deemed "extreme drought." I witnessed animals descending on lower areas in vast numbers. While on a five-day canoeing trip in the Adirondacks, I saw a disproportionate quantity of wildlife concentrated along the banks of the Raquette River, including black bear and white-tailed deer, along with the tracks of coyote and bobcat.

Aquatic life might be confined to shrinking pools, and rising temperatures often create a less-than-hospitable habitat. For land-based animals, drought means a deficit in food, poor hydration, and the crowding of spaces that offer limited resources. Of course, one species' challenge can be another's windfall. As waterways contract, predators that feed on fish, amphibians, and mollusks gain an advantage.

Drought may compel animals to do odd things. Years ago, while I was serving as a guide in the High Peaks of the Adirondacks with my friend Gary, we were sitting in a lean-to at the edge of the Flowed Lands for a well-deserved rest. Our group had gone on a short walk, leaving us with time to chat. This particular year the Flowed Lands were little more than a field of rocks. The forest was dry, and the park agency had enacted a "no fire" policy.

A fisher, presumably on a quest for food, suddenly appeared and began working its way through the pack I had left at the base of a tree not twenty feet away as Gary and I talked. This reclusive mammal was well aware of our presence but seemed almost cavalier about the threat we posed to its well-being. After rooting unsuccessfully through my bag, this typically stealthy predator simply wandered away.

Flooding

On the other end of the spectrum, flooding can displace wildlife and create situations where animals are either forced out of their routines and into the open or, in the case of fish, allowed into areas to which they typically don't have access.

When I was a child living in the suburbs outside of Buffalo, Ellicott Creek flooded on several occasions to devastating levels, leaving neighborhoods waist-deep in coffee-colored water. My friends and I rode our bikes through deep puddles and slogged about on foot through the golf course near my home. I remember chasing carp that had followed the current upstream through the roughs and fairways, and into the shallows of higher ground. We found displaced turtles seeking refuge from the rising waters, wandering as much as a quarter mile from the normally placid creek. Deer grazed in open areas well away from their normal haunts that were too wet to stay in.

Wildfires

Wildfires that occur naturally can actually help to sustain the vibrancy of an ecosystem. As a trail crew volunteer with the Estes-Poudre Ranger District in the summer of 1988, I woke up from a nap after a long night of digging a fire line on a Colorado hillside to see a sage grouse saunter through the charred landscape. This bird seemed remarkably unfazed by the dramatic fire that had ripped through its territory the day before.

When the Montezuma National Wildlife Refuge at the north end of Cayuga Lake experienced a wildfire in 2010, I visited several days later and spoke with a volunteer at the visitor center. She told me that the swallows had feasted on insects that were displaced as grasses, cattails, and sedges burned. She also mentioned that bald eagles, nested in an island of trees at the western rim of the burn area, had seemed unconcerned by the approaching smoke and flames.

With the changes in climate patterns we've seen in the United States over the last two decades, such events are becoming more frequent and consuming more acres. According to the National Interagency Fire Center, since 1960 the three most devastating years for wildfires (in terms of acres lost) were 2015, 2017, and 2020, in what seems unfortunately to be a continuing upward trend. Wildfires do inflict casualties, in the short term as mostly elderly and very young animals are caught in the flames and in the longer term as habitat and food sources are burned, and they cause animals to move, sometimes into areas densely populated by humans. Still, periodic wildfires are a necessary part of natural forest housekeeping.

Weather and Temperature Extremes

Weather and temperature extremes can also impact wildlife and drive animals to behave erratically, forcing them into a state of vulnerability that exceeds the average challenges of seasonal constraints.

One February I traveled to Florida to see my parents and brought a minimum of warm clothing, expecting balmy afternoons and humid nights. But I awoke on the morning of my first full day to a frigid temperature of 27 degrees Fahrenheit. My father had planned an outdoor adventure to Blue Spring State Park in Volusia County, a famous manatee preserve. Outside of the occasional televised nature program, I had never seen a manatee and was eager to go. What I didn't know is that manatees are temperature sensitive and prone to hypothermia. This cold snap worked to our benefit—a huge number of manatees had retreated to the warmth of the park's springs off the Saint Johns River. I went from never having seen a manatee to observing more than two hundred in one day. The 72-degree water that filled the springs offered these docile giants a refuge from the comparatively cold waters of the nearby river.

Years later, in the fall of 2012, Hurricane Sandy crept up the Eastern Seaboard. In upstate New York, the sky swirled with sinister clouds. One thing I unexpectedly observed on the afternoon of October 29 was a flight of cormorants. These diving seabirds have long resided in the Great Lakes. With their dark bodies and serpentine necks, they are easy to identify. Our local population, however, prefers to sit in the branches of old cottonwoods at the south end of Cayuga Lake. I had never seen them venture from the shores of the lake and its adjoining tributaries, but on the day Hurricane Sandy made landfall, hundreds of cormorants flew over Ithaca's Fall Creek neighborhood. They circled back and forth, seeking more protection than the exposed lakeshore could provide.

Exercises

- Recognizing and understanding animal vulnerabilities involves a fundamental shift in perspective. Begin by asking yourself essential questions when observing wildlife, including: Is this animal at a point in its yearly cycle when it is in a heightened state of defenselessness? Research how the original human inhabitants of your region made use of these vulnerabilities.

- Attempt to "intercept" an animal by using your awareness of its vulnerabilities. For example, a shallow creek may offer increased access to fish during a summertime drought. But be respectful of dens and nests—these are places best observed from a distance.

- How do birds that nest on the ground differ from birds that nest in trees in their approach to thwarting predatory vulnerabilities? What do you think might be the reasons for these differences? Is one approach more effective than the other, or is each suited to the demands of its particular habitat?

CHAPTER 6

Tracks and Sign

Time and again you come upon the isolated
and succinct evidence of life—animal tracks,
the undigested remains of a ptarmigan in
an owl's casting, a patch of barren-ground
willow nibbled nearly lifeless by arctic hares.

—BARRY LOPEZ, *ARCTIC DREAMS*

My friend Sean Cornell calls to me through the forest:
"Hey, Dave! I think we have fisher tracks!" We're in the
throes of a winter survival intensive course and have already
been surprised with the tracks of a bobcat. Trailing this elusive feline is
a first for us in these woods.

I've been leading Primitive Pursuits groups in this mixed-age forest for almost two decades, so this new track is cause for celebration. Near the hill at the state forest boundary, anything and everything you might expect to discover can be found—bear, fisher, bobcat, and sometimes otter in the wetlands below. Down in the valley, an area dominated by farmland, there are fox, coyote, and smaller predators that make their home near the fringes of these woods.

The fisher is another first. After finishing up some projects, we split our group in half. Sean's team follows the tracks through a dusting of snow toward a pine forest, while my group backtracks in the other direction.

I've followed fisher tracks through the woods enough to not be surprised by this one's meandering, curious path. It leads us over logs and through tight spots, as we investigate every nook and tangle. Unlike the wild canines of the area, whose trails are comparatively businesslike, the fisher will sometimes stop and loop back on itself.

As we follow the tracks through the thin snow, we discover this particular member of the weasel family has come through a thicket that was once a farm field. As fishers reclaim territory and increase their range, we have learned that their comfort zone is much more expansive than previously thought. Once relegated to the deep wilderness, this highly adaptable animal is now willing to skirt along the edges of humanity and take advantage, much like raccoons, of some of the resources available in these environments. By tracking this animal we learn that its numbers are likely increasing as it spreads out across the land and that it can thrive in a variety of habitats.

Tracking is a process that forces you to look beyond the surface and ask questions. As your skills improve and your awareness expands, your knowledge and instincts will become more reliable.

The Art of Tracking

Tracking, in its essence, is the art of finding and evaluating evidence of activity, including footprints, trail patterns, odors, markings, shelter, and signs such as hair, scat, chews, bones, kills, or feeding sites. Successful tracking often involves ruling out possibilities. Armed with a reliable field guide and a willingness to take time with the details, you more often than not can determine a track's maker.

Take your time. Don't try and put a name on anything unless you're certain of its origin; collect evidence and make a list of the most

---

PREVIOUS IMAGE I discovered these bobcat tracks in fresh snow near my home. This once rare animal has rebounded very well in New York State and has found opportunities in a great variety of habitats.

Tracking

Here are a few of my favorite books on tracking:

- *Animal Tracking Basics* by Tiffany Morgan and Jon Young
- *Animal Tracks* by Olaus Murie, Peterson Field Guides
- *Animal Tracks: Midwest Edition* by Jonathan Poppele
- *A Field Guide to Tracking Mammals in the Northeast* by Linda J. Spielman
- *Mammal Tracks and Sign of the Northeast* by Dianne Gibbons
- *Scats and Tracks of the Midwest* by James Halfpenny
- *The Science and Art of Tracking* by Tom Brown Jr.
- *Tom Brown's Field Guide to Nature Observation and Tracking* by Tom Brown Jr. with Brandt Morgan
- *Tracking and the Art of Seeing* by Paul Rezendes

These guides, written by experts in the field, provide an array of perspectives. I am particularly fond of *Mammal Tracks and Sign of the Northeast*. It takes you through a series of questions that will lead you to the correct answer. You may need to research the best field guides or keys for your geographic region.

likely candidates. It's better to admit uncertainty and list reasonable prospects than to proclaim something that might be inaccurate. Above all, be humble, meaning recognize that you are on a journey to connect with and better understand nature and that this process can take time. It is okay not to know right away; answers will come with patience, good questions, and observation.

"Never memorize something you can look up" is a saying often attributed to Albert Einstein. He didn't actually say this but still I have always found solace in this piece of wisdom. In my own experiences with tracking, I often struggle to remember things such as numbers

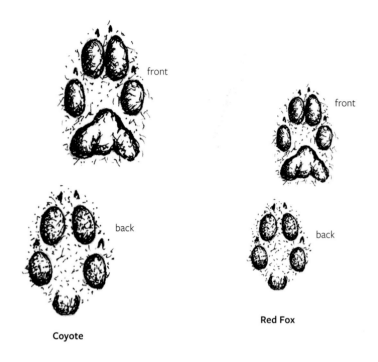

front

front

back

back

Red Fox

Coyote

Although the tracks of coyotes and red fox are very similar—each having four toes with claws visible—the observant tracker will come to see distinct differences in such things as size, shape, and stride.

of toes, average stride length, and the specifics of foot measurement. Unlike some of my fellow naturalists who seem to have an encyclopedic knowledge of such things, I more often turn to field guides. Fortunately, there are more than a few excellent books on tracking, to which I frequently refer. A list of other valuable resources is included at the end of this book.

Much like how an ornithologist looks for field marks to properly identify birds, the tracker must key in to certain clues. *Mammal Tracks and Sign of the Northeast* by Dianne Gibbons works on this premise—by examining the specifics of a clear print, you can determine a track's origin (assuming you're in the Northeast, that is). To the trained eye, the field marks of a coyote, for example, are far different from those of a red fox. Even though both canines have four toes on their front and back feet with claw marks, their tracks show striking dissimilarities. This brings us to a discussion of footprints and impressions.

Footprints and Impressions

I can't possibly begin to recreate the vast stores of information that have been documented in texts solely dedicated to the art of tracking. Instead, I intend to open your mind to the potential that the practice offers and present exercises that will help you navigate the often-precarious realm of track identification.

Let's begin by delving into the process of identification. Ideally, you're looking for a clear and complete print or series of prints. In most situations—outside of model substrate such as damp snow, wet sand, clay, or mud—finding a print that displays all of the important details can be difficult.

Discovering a clear print, especially for the novice tracker, is essential to ensure you have all of the correct information to narrow down your choices. Better still is finding a series of tracks: you will be able to measure stride and determine the average distance between steps. In many situations, if the prints are unclear, knowing the variations in gait or stride within a specific family (for example, that a red fox's average stride is shorter than a coyote's) will be useful.

The process I typically go through to identify a track begins with generalities and moves toward specifics. I have included a simple yet effective chart to help you narrow down your choices to the proper group or family by comparing the number of toes on the front and back feet.

Asking straightforward questions based on close observation is the first step in determining potential suspects. Felines and canines, for example, whether domestic or wild, all have four toes with claw marks on both the front and back feet. But cats have retractable claws that rarely show in their roundish prints, making them relatively easy to distinguish from the dog family.

Once you have firmly established the family, narrow your search using at least one reliable field guide and a ruler. Depending on the field guide you use, it is often helpful (but not essential) to know an animal's family.

The field marks of a track are hidden in the details of each species' foot. The white-tailed deer and mule deer, for example, are both herbivores from the same family and therefore leave similar prints. But it is the details in the field marks that delineate the differences between the two and make it possible to identify the source. (The term *field mark*, though often used to describe an animal's physical characteristics, here refers to the distinguishing features of a track.)

It is easier to identify a particular species if you are familiar with its geographic location. Lynxes, for example, were at one time native to upstate New York, but because of trapping, logging, and urbanization, they have been driven north of the Canadian border. If I encounter a track that looks like it might belong to a lynx, I can rule out that possibility because of where I live.

With birds, it is important to note that as a general rule, tree dwellers (like the chickadee) hop on both feet while ground dwellers (like the wild turkey) walk in an alternating pattern. Because lightweight songbirds may not leave tracks except in mud or snow, look instead for remnants of seeds or berries. Also be aware of feathers or, with owls and other birds of prey, regurgitated pellets.

In the Northeast, tracking is most difficult in the fall because of changing leaf cover. By contrast, winter snow makes tracking easier. The quality of a track is often determined by weather, wind (direction, angle, and velocity), erosion, and soil type. An animal's weight is also a factor. Some substrates are far less ideal than others. Loamy soil, made up of decaying leaves and pine needles, is so spongy that it will often bounce back after a track is made.

Be sure to look not only at tracks but also the stories they tell: their orientation, starts, and stops. For example, a deer's dewclaws (vestigial digits) usually register only when they are running. (On occasion they may also register when the deer is walking on a soft substrate where footing is poor.) Might the presence of dewclaws indicate a disturbance? Is there a predator afoot? Always ask yourself these types of questions when tracking.

This is a track from an eastern timber wolf, found along the edge of Loughrin Creek in Algonquin Provincial Park, Ontario, Canada.

Baseline Movement Patterns: Gait and Stride

When tracks are unclear because of poor substrate (such as melting snow), the tracker is left only with patterns. Each species has a baseline movement pattern, a gait that conserves energy and is ultimately a safer way to negotiate the landscape. (A slow-moving animal is less likely to be detected by predators than an animal that is moving quickly.) The ability to recognize patterns will help you narrow down your choices. And by comparing strides, you can begin to determine a track's origin. Cats and dogs, for example, are both diagonal walkers, but through the measurement of stride and trail width you can whittle down your list of probable suspects.

Although experts do not have an agreed-upon or universal terminology for describing track patterns, most use some typical ones,

Family	Track Shape	Toes front	Toes rear	Claws?
Cat		4	4	No
Dog		4	4	Yes
Rabbit & Hare		4	4	Maybe
Rodent	back front	4	5	Usually
Armadillo	back front	4	5	Yes
Mustelid Family (mink, weasels, badger, otter, fisher, wolverine)	back front	5	5	Usually
Shrew		5	5	Yes
Procyonids (raccoon, white-nosed coati, ringtail)	back front	5	5	Yes
Bear		5	5	Yes
Opossum	back front	5	5	Yes
Deer		Hoof	Hoof	N/A

Compression shape	Toes	Larger foot	Normal gait
Round	Round or teardrop	Front	Diagonal walker
Oval or rectangle	Oval	Front	Diagonal walker
Exclamation point or mushroom cap	Indistinct	Rear	Galloper
2-thumb mitten	Long & thin	Same	Galloper/pacer
Oval	Long & thin	Hind	Pacer
Sideways rectangle or oval; rear feet of big weasels are ice-cream-cone shaped	Round or teardrop	Same	Bounder
Oval	Round or oval; often very hard to see because of small size.	Same	Pacer
Plantigrade u-shaped at back from heel	Elongated, oval, or finger-like	Raccoon: Rear larger because more heel register	2 x 2 (raccoon), overstep (white-nosed coati), walk/ bound (ringtail)
Plantigrade u-shaped at back from heel	Oval	Rear larger because more heel register	Pacer
Plantigrade u-shaped at back from heel	Finger-like	Rear larger because more heel register	Under-step walker
Heart-shaped	N/A	Same	Diagonal walker

including diagonal walking (cats, dogs, hoofed mammals, beavers, and porcupines); galloping (rabbits, hares, and rodents); bounding (weasels, fishers, minks); and pacing (bears, opossums, and raccoons). As a reminder, animals move in a variety of ways depending on the situation. The appearance and spacing of deer tracks, for example, will fluctuate depending on whether the animal is at rest or in flight. Deer walk in a diagonal or alternating baseline pattern but alter their gait as their speed increases. What's most essential is the ability to describe and understand, by looking at the tracks, how an animal is moving—a challenging but rewarding pursuit.

Sign Tracking and Field Marks

Beyond footprints and impressions, animals put down an array of sign. As an animal undertakes its life-supporting behaviors, it leaves all manner of clues that reveal not only its presence but also specific information about what it's been doing. This evidence of activity is sometimes more revealing than footprints.

One day while walking through the forest, a friend and I noticed several owl pellets. (These regurgitated remains provide wonderful clues about an owl's diet and whereabouts.) As we continued on, we identified other areas where pellets had been deposited. Like old-school detectives, we followed the trail to the base of a tall oak. There, perched on a branch fifty feet above us, was a great horned owl. I regularly spotted this particular owl, which was in a tract of woods near the University of Buffalo, once I learned which trees it preferred for roosting.

In late spring and early summer I always look for the telltale signs of snapping turtle activity: digging. At the Jim Schug Trail in Dryden,

Scent left by a beaver near the shores of Cayuga Lake, New York

New York, which follows an abandoned railroad bed through a vast wetland, I've seen as many as a half dozen females laying their eggs on either side of the path at once. Driven by instinct, this incredible reptile is compelled to do what turtles have been doing since the late Triassic period—leave the safety of the water to deposit its clutch on land. The laying of eggs in the hope of reproducing a new generation of snappers is not a conscious choice but a function of biology. Even when turtles are not physically present, their actions leave behind obvious, unmistakable sign. These nests, typically dug into open, sunny areas, are easy to locate, but they often offer an easy meal for opportunistic raccoons. Raided nests are usually littered with the leathery remains of embryonic life.

Many of the behaviors discussed in Chapter 4 involve corresponding physical evidence that a tracker can look for, such as hair, feathers, scat, chews, bones, kill or feeding sites, odors, markings, and shelter. Other field marks include the following:

- **Trails, runs, and escape routes.** Paths of all stripes are a great place to look for prints. These also offer the potential for additional clues, including where an animal sleeps, what it eats, and where it finds water.
- **Territories.** Look for clues that indicate an animal's territory. Indicators can include scent posts, buck rubs and scrapes, dens, and nests.
- **Sheltering and resting sites.** Pay attention to where an animal chooses to rest; these spots often directly correlate with preferred habitats. These are also good areas to look for hair and prints.
- **Indications of communication and elimination.** Look for strategically placed scat, urine, and scent posts. Scat will also help you determine what an animal has been eating—providing some indication of resident prey species.
- **Indications of ingesting.** Look for things such as kill sites, owl pellets, scat, browse, digs, and storage sites. Squirrels, for example, may keep larders to anticipate upcoming seasonal needs.

During the writing of this book, a young beaver my family named Merle showed up at the small pond on our property. He had likely been forced to leave his birth home and find his own place. This migration of sorts is a very dangerous time for young beavers. They often travel well away from water or move through shallow waterways to find a suitable location. At best, our pond was an adequate (but by no means ideal) beaver habitat—the stream that flows into and out of this reservoir generally dries up in the summer, and the pond itself had been quietly shrinking as it filled with sediment over the years. A recent flood had eroded the spillway, shrinking the pond even further.

Despite the less-than-optimal conditions, this beaver found his way to our small oasis and decided to set up shop. In short order he

Beavers are incredibly fun and rewarding animals to observe and track. These large rodents leave a great variety of sign around their watery homes, including chewed sticks, scent mounds, trails, fallen trees, dams, and a shelter of some sort. Usually this dwelling is a lodge surrounded by water, but sometimes beavers make an "invisible" home, which is a den dug into a bank.

brought the pond up to historic levels by damming the main berm over which the waters had started to spill. My family and I had the honor of experiencing the life of a solitary beaver up close for a full year.

In addition to a prized front-row seat (he was amazingly tolerant of our presence, allowing us to sit at the fringe of the wetland as he preened, ate, and swam about), each morning I was treated to evidence of his nightly activities: saplings that had been cut down and brought to the pond's edge; the dam growing more substantial; and piles of bark-stripped sticks. I could tell by their absence that he also appreciated the apples I'd left behind. (I'll discuss Merle and the issue of habituating animals to human contact in Chapter 9.)

Your Tracking Journal

Tracking is all about process—a process that leads you to ask questions such as, How can I tell the difference between similar animals by comparing their tracks? One thing that will prove useful is to keep a tracking journal and illustrate confusing tracks near each other for side-by-side comparison. Be sure to note track diameter, relationship of toes to heel pads, and average stride lengths and trail patterns. Include in this journal any sign you encounter, such as hair or feathers, which can be taped to a page. (Botanists may also want to include leaves.) Also be sure to note the time of day, location, environment, and any other details you find pertinent.

Let's use wild canines to demonstrate how this works. In the northeastern United States we have red fox and gray fox, eastern coyote, and domestic (and sometimes feral) dogs. All of these animals show four toes in the front and four in the back with claws. By creating a journal wherein you draw each species' individual tracks along with average stride lengths, you will come to learn the subtle and sometimes not-so-subtle differences between species.

I encourage the use of a pencil and paper as your primary way of recording and learning about your discoveries as opposed to simply taking a picture with your smartphone and using an app. By looking very closely and then drawing all of the details that culminate to create the particular track in front of you, you will be engaged in a much more significant way than you would be in the relatively quick act of taking a snapshot with your phone.

A tracking or nature journal is an indispensable tool that can record far more than tracks with descriptive text and measurements. A few things to include in this journal are:

Journals serve as a valuable tool that allow you to collect data and record experiences. Over time they will reveal patterns and help unravel wildlife mysteries.

MINK - (MUSTELA VISON)   ENTRY 12/19/21

MANY MINK HAVE BEEN SPOTTED IN THE LAST
6 MONTHS. EVERY ANIMAL WAS SEEN IN'S
AROUND WATER INCLUDING LAKE CHAMPLAIN,
MUD LOCK, CAYUGA LAKE, THE INLET ; FALL CK.
I HAVE DISCOVERED SEVERAL "HOT SPOTS" IN
STEWART PARK ALONG THE POND ; CREEK
EDGE. THE MINK @ THE DOWNED WILLOW
IN THE POND HAS BEEN SEEN MARKING
MANY TIMES. GOOD MINK SPOTS REMIND ME OF
GOOD SPOTS TO FISH FOR BASS. LIKE BASS
MINK LIKE COVER, BOTH IN'S OUT OF THE
WATER, SUCH AS ROCK PILES ; TIMBER THAT
HAS FALLEN 〰

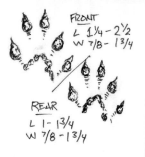

FRONT
L 1¼ - 2½
W ⅞ - 1¾

REAR
L 1 - 1¾
W ⅞ - 1¾

TRACKS SEEN IN
MUD AT WATERS
EDGE BY BOATHOUSE

RECENT SIGHTINGS —
11/20 – 12:30 P.M.
11/22   1:20 P.M.
12/2   10:15 AM
12/15   12:45 P.M.

ALL DATES – FINE,
FAIR WEATHER W/
SUN —
MINK OBSERVED
HUNTING, RESTING,
MARKING ;
WATCHING ME AS
I OBSERVED THEM.

THINGS TO INVESTIGATE

* SIZE OF TERRITORY
* BREEDING ; YOUNG
* RANGE
* PREY / PREDATORS
* DENNING
* COMFORT W/ PEOPLE
* VOCALIZATIONS

* MARKING

SIMILAR TRACKS

* FISHER
* MARTEN
* WEASLE

- stride and baseline movement patterns and measurements, especially valuable when prints are unclear
- common gait patterns within a species
- a rough sketch of the animal in question
- physical evidence (hairs or feathers taped to the page, for example)
- any natural history or other field notes that you find helpful
- location
- date and time of day
- weather

Ultimately, it is up to you to decide how to organize your journal. Make it useful and practical.

Exercises

○ Begin by tracking in an easy-to-mark substrate (such as mud) and learn to recognize the differences between animal families. (Setting up a "tracking box" with damp sand is also useful. Damp sand has the wonderful quality of holding the details of a track. If you want, once you have finished examining the most recent recordings, you can smooth over the sand and make it ready for the next animal to come by.) Once you can easily identify a member of the cat family, for example, you can then move on to determine the specific species within that family.

○ Get in the habit of seeing the whole picture when it comes to tracking. Look *beyond* the track and ask how such things as habitat, topography, and food availability affect which creatures you might encounter.

○ A fun activity that can be done with clay is track creation. Each person attempts to create a lifelike track using clay, putty, or other flexible materials. Once everyone has completed their track, the leader mixes up the tracks and passes them back randomly to the group. The hope is that the track has been represented well and that each person will be able to accurately identify the track they have.

CHAPTER 7

Calling and Influencing Animals

. . . in nature nothing exists alone.

—RACHEL CARSON, *SILENT SPRING*

During my adolescence, my family often vacationed on Sanibel Island in southwestern Florida. Home to the J.N. "Ding" Darling National Wildlife Refuge and with access to the Gulf of Mexico as well as opportunities to experience Florida's backwaters, Sanibel is a magical place with ample wild spaces. During a fishing trip in this unique habitat, I unintentionally learned something about calling alligators.

As I walked along a recreation trail frequented by hikers, cyclists, and the occasional gopher tortoise, I made my way to a small marsh hoping to catch largemouth bass. I cast toward the opposite bank with my crankbait, dropping my lure at the edge of the sawgrass, and began to gently tease the line. The lure I used was designed to quiver like a small fish as I reeled it in. I often like to let lures of this type rest on the surface for a moment before retrieving them, giving them a faint twitch in the hope of enticing a fish.

Without warning, a small alligator surfaced and swam toward the ripples my bait had created. Not wanting to hook this two-foot-long reptile, I reeled in to cast in another direction. But with each new attempt, the gator swam toward my lure. Despite my best efforts to the contrary, he crossed my line and I accidentally hooked him in the foot. An epic battle ensued.

For forty-five minutes I struggled to bring the alligator to shore to attempt to remove the hook. I eventually reeled him into the sawgrass where the line snapped, setting him free.

My unintended "calling" of a small crocodilian is but one example of a practice that can be used in a variety of ways. The alligator in question was drawn to the disturbance I created, presumably under the impression that there was prey in distress. Other animals I have influenced over the years include owls (screech, barred, and great horned), turkeys, songbirds, hawks, spiders, deer, raccoons, squirrels (both red and gray), chipmunks, mice, rabbits, bats, crows, fish, fishers, snakes, crayfish, beavers, tree frogs, foxes (both red and gray), snapping turtles, woodchucks, black bears (unintentionally), and a second alligator (this one on purpose).

The Nature of Calling

Calling is a universal art found across both traditional and contemporary cultures. It provides a visual cue, odor, taste, vibration, sound, or opportunity that piques an animal's curiosity and appeals to inherent needs. (Though there are animal senses that extend beyond normal human capacity, such as echolocation, here we will focus on methods of calling that can be employed fairly easily.) The practice

PREVIOUS IMAGE All animals can be influenced or called in one or more ways. Over time, as an animal's needs, fears, vocalizations, and habits are discovered, the thoughtful naturalist can utilize this knowledge to affect the choices of wildlife.

This traditional turkey call is made from the wing bones of a turkey.

involves understanding an animal so intimately that you can influence its behavior. By appealing to an animal's sense of hunger, its drive to reproduce, or the need to defend its territory, skilled naturalists increase their chances of not only viewing wildlife but also getting it to do what they want.

Before embarking on a study of calling, be sure to consider all of the elements an animal needs to survive and the numerous behaviors described in Chapter 4 that offer potential arenas for influence. Be willing to experiment, test theories, and try out various approaches to this topic. In the modern world, for example, most of us are familiar with feeding birds. This innocent and enjoyable hobby is, in fact, a form of calling. Knowing that birds need to eat in order to survive, you can place a feeder in a way that all but guarantees the intended result. All too often, unfortunately, people today leave a trail of food and other resources without having any idea they are influencing animals. Being deliberate in your calling will help make you more responsible toward and alert to the wildlife around you.

As a reminder, be sure to avoid causing unnecessary disturbance or stress to wildlife. If you influence animals and birds to come closer, do it in responsible ways. These points from the "Guidelines for Thoughtful Engagement" in Chapter 1 particularly apply:

· Be considerate of rare species, species of concern, or species that live in sensitive habitats.
· Remain sensitive to seasonal pressures.
· Consider the time of year if you choose to call. In winter, some birds, for example, may have a limited food supply and may be operating with a very small energy reserve.

Life Cycle and Manipulation

Animal behavior can be influenced in a variety of ways. Predator calls, scents, and decoys can be purchased for use in hunting and fishing, and these tools can be useful in nature observation as well. But in observing wildlife I prefer to rely on techniques and resources that I can produce on my own. As always, the weather, time of day, and the animal's yearly cycle must all be taken into consideration.

Calling and manipulation are most often employed during specific parts of an animal's life cycle, including times when the animal is defending territory, striving to reproduce, rearing young, seeking shelter and habitat, and hunting or foraging. Calling can also take advantage of an animal's instinct to stay safe and alive by paying attention to alarm calls.

Defending Territory

The discussion in Chapter 4 of courtship behaviors mentioned male-to-male aggression as it relates to the importance of finding adequate space for nesting and the rearing of young. The fundamental question for animals at this point in their yearly cycle is whether they have established the territory and resources necessary to ensure continuation of the species. Researchers often employ calling to draw male birds out of hiding, tricking them into believing that another male has invaded their territory. Be forewarned, though: if you pretend to be a competing male in an established male's territory, you will often elicit an aggressive response from your intended quarry.

I once observed a Cooper's hawk as it soared over an open lawn, flew across a road, and then circled around an old farmhouse before landing in a tree. To determine if it was a male, I offered my best Cooper's hawk call. This crow-sized accipiter suddenly dropped from its resting place and sailed toward me. For a moment I thought I was going to get buzzed by the raptor until a car pulled into the parking lot where I was standing and scared it off. The hawk made a quick southward turn and disappeared.

Near the end of a spring backpacking trip, I paused with my Primitive Pursuits group to rest on a snow-covered trail in Hammond

Barred owls range most typically in the eastern half of the United States but can also be found in southern Canada and parts of the Pacific Northwest. Mimicking the call of a barred owl at the right time of day may prompt any that are nearby to fly closer.

Hill State Forest in Dryden, New York. Without warning, a barred owl call rang out from the trees. While the remainder of the group enjoyed a brief respite, two participants who were interested in seeing if they could spot this elusive bird of prey joined me and we ventured into the woods.

We crept off trail, and one of us offered a convincing imitation of the owl's cry, bellowing out a throaty, "Who cooks for you? Who cooks for you all?" at regular intervals. We heard it respond a few times but weren't rewarded with a glimpse. Thinking that our attempt to court the bird was ineffective, we worked our way back toward the main trail to rejoin the group.

What we discovered was that the call had indeed brought in an owl, but not the one we were pursuing. To our surprise, a second owl had been drawn out of the forest from the opposite direction and landed on a branch near the resting group.

As always, use this technique mindfully and sparingly to avoid thoughtlessly stressing an animal. Introducing a foreign odor might also draw out wildlife to defend their territory, since scent posts often determine territorial boundaries.

Striving to Reproduce

The drive to reproduce often supplants all other needs and diminishes an animal's focus on awareness, invisibility, and safety. The attentive naturalist can use scent, visual cues, or sound to influence wildlife that are vulnerable to such ploys during mating season. For example, bucks are drawn to doe urine when they are looking for a mate, so bow hunters sometimes use a commercially available product to draw a curious buck within range. Mimicking buck grunts, doe bleats, and the rattling of antlers is a common approach to draw unsuspecting deer into range for observing. Always keep in mind that large herbivores can be dangerous; do not use these techniques without caution and consideration.

Rearing Young

Appealing to parental instincts is another way to manipulate wildlife, although it is not commonly employed to call in animals. I am admittedly uncomfortable with the idea of concerning a parent by taking advantage of its devotion to its offspring. This aspect of calling should be used with great discretion since healthy wildlife populations depend on parents finding safe places to rear their offspring. Although I have succeeded with this approach on more than one occasion, I use it sparingly, generally only to test out a new situation or theory.

One quiet afternoon I made my way along a trail at the base of the Appalachian Ridge in New Jersey. The path led me through dense undergrowth thick with greenbrier, rose, and other fruity scrub. As I continued on, the woods opened up to a view of a white-tailed doe calmly grazing about seventy-five yards away. Curious as to whether a fawnlike call would provoke any sort of response, I squatted with my back against a large maple and let out a mournful bleat.

Fawns sometimes make a "bleat" call much like that of a lamb. This sound, mimicked and emitted at the right time of year, can draw in nearby does. (iStock/szixy)

The doe seemed oblivious and soon disappeared from view. For fifteen minutes I sat still, periodically reproducing this plaintive distress call. I almost gave up, figuring my imitation wasn't credible or that this supposed technique was only a myth. Then, without warning, she emerged not ten feet from my location. Because I had taken no measures to de-scent, the shifting breeze immediately prompted her to flee. This event took place in the spring when fawns were new, and appealing to this maternal instinct was more likely to be effective. Outside of the proper season, this kind of calling can seem suspicious and prove ineffective.

Seeking Shelter and Habitat

Once properly identified, an active nest or den is an excellent place to observe the comings and goings of wildlife. As previously stated, a den or nest—especially one teeming with young—can and should be viewed through the lens of vulnerability. In such cases, calling should not be used.

Beyond discovering an animal's nest or den, the motivated naturalist can influence where an animal chooses to live by creating or

providing such places if they are not readily available within the landscape. Providing birdhouses, brush piles, or more elaborate shelters is an enriching way to ensure diversity. The screech owl house mounted on the south side of my barn is used by gray squirrels. I don't mind that the grays have moved in. They are fun to watch, and I look forward to seeing if the owl house remains the best choice to raise a litter of squirrel pups. I'll put up another box or two in different locations and see if one of them attracts the intended species.

Very often animals use and take advantage of human infrastructure, with exciting results. One spring I was invited to the home of an acquaintance to observe a family of red foxes that had taken up residence under her garden shed. (I have come to believe the choice to live in close proximity to humankind is often deliberate. In the Northeast, where the eastern coyote population has grown significantly, a red fox's decision to den near humans can help ensure its safety.) As I

Pollinator Pathways

Pollinator Pathways (pollinator-pathway.org) is an organization that helps educate the public on plants that can be established in backyards and urban areas to help provide "pollinator-friendly habitats and food sources for bees, butterflies, hummingbirds, and other pollinating insects and wildlife." Pathways of pesticide-free native plants cobbled together from public and private spaces provide greater benefits to pollinators than isolated patches.

Humans can help hummingbirds by planting flowers that provide nectar. (iStock/Karel Bock)

sat comfortably in my host's dining room, one adorable fox kit after another emerged from beneath the shed to groom and bask in the sun.

It's important to remember that the attuned naturalist can manage any property under his or her stewardship for the benefit of wildlife. Habitat help may include building rock piles, planting or cutting trees, and creating funnels to direct animal traffic. Funnels are a simple way to direct an animal a certain direction or down a specific trail. For example, in winter when we have deep snow, I will pack down a trail leading from a nearby rabbit den to wherever I want it to lead them. These trails immediately become used as it is easier for our resident cottontails to travel on packed-down snow than on powder snow.

I am quite selective about the trees I choose for firewood and often manage forested areas on my land in such a way that they continue to provide nuts, fruits, and homes for wildlife. I rarely remove snags, or standing deadwood, because of their immense value as a habitat for insects and homes for an assortment of birds and mammals. I have also purposely kept our fields open. These offer transition areas and a variety of foraging opportunities in a landscape dominated by forest. In recent years I have even begun to create brush piles to attract wildlife. This new and rewarding pursuit was prompted by a discovery I made while tracking a wounded deer through my neighbor's property. As I walked through the melting snow I encountered a variety of rabbit sign including tracks, scat, and browse. My property, despite being less than a half mile away, was virtually free of rabbits. The difference, I realized, was shelter.

My neighbor's land was completely disheveled, to the obvious benefit of rabbits. The property was riddled with old log piles, decaying outbuildings, and an array of scrub that aided the eastern cottontail in a multitude of ways. Since this discovery, I have made it a point to create brush piles from the top portions of trees that I've culled for firewood. The results are almost always immediate, a veritable field of dreams for wildlife: if you build it, they will come.

Hunting or Foraging

Many of us have put out bird food, such as suet for woodpeckers or nectar for hummingbirds, making us familiar with baiting to draw an animal to a desired location. Baiting—offering animals something they desire that isn't readily accessible at a certain time of year—takes advantage of an animal's year-round need to feed itself and offers great opportunity to influence an animal's behavior.

But baiting isn't synonymous with simply placing a food source in a promising location; you can also take advantage of an existing situation. A deer carcass, for example, will draw in all manner of forest residents. Near my home, I have tracked the comings and goings of fishers, raccoons, mice, and squirrels, as well as all the species of birds that benefit from plundering a dead animal. In my neighborhood, the array of seasonal food sources includes spring succulents, cherries, apples, and acorns. The ability to identify food sources (coupled with knowing the dietary preferences of your local inhabitants) will go a long way toward recognizing "active positions" in the landscape. Think of it as discovering the seasonal larders in your area and noticing which animals take advantage of their bounty.

Deliberate baiting with wild offerings is a specialty that takes time and dedication to master. Baiting is often associated with traditional trapping but it doesn't have to have lethal implications. I have experimented with a variety of natural lures, including apples, fish entrails, and gut piles. Bait can be placed near good substrate that will hold an animal's tracks, or you can use a camera with a motion sensor to see who has visited. If you have the patience, you can just conceal yourself nearby with a camera and wait to see who comes in for the offering.

Several winters ago, after one of our laying hens died, I decided to suspend her from a branch to see what I could bring in. Every few days I checked my trail camera to see what, if anything, had come to visit. The area was devoid of activity for almost a month. Apparently a frozen, feathered chicken didn't put off enough odor for our local predators to notice.

I relayed my story to my friend and traditional skills master Justin Sutera, and he suggested I try some beaver castor. The castor gland secretes a yellowish liquid that when combined with urine is used to mark and establish a beaver's territory. It is remarkably pungent. I decided to give it a shot. I took some castor from a beaver that Justin had legally trapped and put some of it on a log near the chicken. The effects were immediate. That first night, two raccoons were rewarded with a meal of frozen poultry. The second night brought in a fisher. And the following night a curious doe stopped by to investigate.

It became clear that rich, heady odors offer the best chance for success, particularly in colder climates. This doesn't mean that concentrations of fruits, nuts, seeds, or berries should be avoided, only that these may require more thoughtful placement to be effective. I have attracted deer into my baiting schemes using wild apples; they are often quite willing to pluck fruit from a well-placed bait stick.

On a more whimsical note, one afternoon my eldest son, Jacob, and I were able to use earthworms to prompt our resident wild garter snake, Helen, to action. After collecting a handful of large specimens from our compost heap, Jacob stalked toward the basking snake. With

Scent and Curiosity

For many animals, their olfactory system informs them about the world more than any other sense. Strategically placed odors (food, urine, scat, or glandular secretions) can be used to attract (or in some cases, repel) a multitude of animals. Scents can appeal to a creature's general curiosity, reproductive drive, or need for sustenance.

My friend Bob Berg of Thunderbird Atlatl once mentioned a simple way to draw in white-tailed deer: simply push leaves away from an area on the forest floor to reveal fresh earth. Once when I was out in a local forest, while not even thinking of Bob's technique, I moved some dry leaves from a spot where I'd chosen to stand. Though I didn't see any deer, I returned the following afternoon to discover that a deer had in fact walked and then stood directly in the place where I had spent many hours the day before. This area was not on an established thoroughfare, and it seemed more than coincidental; the deer was very likely intrigued by the smell of fresh soil.

blue heron–like patience he slowly lowered a dangling earthworm over her head. When Jacob's hand reached a distance of about two feet from Helen, she took notice of the twitching worm that was magically suspended above her. She then rose up and gently took the worm from Jacob's fingers.

Staying Safe and Alive

As we have already learned, animals are vigilant and have an incentive to stay safe and alive by paying attention to the behaviors and reactions around them. Creating fictitious alarms can have dramatic effects.

"Pishing" is a method of mimicry that is employed for the purpose of drawing songbirds into open areas for observation. This generic alarming communicates the message that something in the environment is awry. Concerned birds are drawn toward the alarm

I successfully call in a large female garter snake who used to bask in the sun outside of our home. Despite having one eye, she got along well as she lived out her life alongside ours.

to identify the threat and then take the proper action to stay safe. Pete Dunne's *The Art of Pishing* is a wonderful resource on this arcane topic; the book comes with an audio CD to assist readers in producing the desired call.

On numerous occasions I have witnessed blue jays use mimicry to their advantage. While on a walk on a golf course one winter day in suburban North Carolina, I heard the calls of a red-shouldered hawk. Looking toward a large backyard tree, I discovered a jay mimicking the call of the common raptor. This common ruse puts nearby birds on alert. In this instance, the jay cleared away all competition from an open feeder and had it all to itself. Often jays reinforce the ruse by letting out a few alarm calls of their own. I have wondered how long this scheme can go on before the other birds catch on.

Use of Decoys

Decoys or visual cues can be used to attract animals by playing upon many arenas of an animal's life, including socializing, threat, courtship, and mating rites. The use of decoys is familiar to hunters of native waterfowl, but it can also be leveraged for naturalist observation. Decoys are often used in situations where visual cues are crucial. For instance, placing a raft of artificial ducks on the water can encourage airborne birds to land nearby, as the decoys indicate that the area is safe and the feeding is good.

I have witnessed and used decoys in a variety of ways over the years. One of my more exciting decoy-related exploits involved a spontaneous encounter with a gray fox. One summer evening, my wife and I were sitting on the deck of our apartment when a gray fox trotted into the yard. Mimicking a classic technique in which researchers catch great horned owls by "fishing" for them in the woods (a rodent lure is drawn through the leaf litter, thereby drawing these birds of prey into a net), I hastily tied a sock to the end of my fishing line and prepared to cast.

Our elevated deck offered the perfect vantage for peering into the yard. My cast was a bit off and my line landed draped over the branch of a small tree, leaving the sock dangling just above the grass. I gave the line a few twitches that immediately brought the fox in to investigate. My wife and I did our best to suppress our laughter as the fox leapt about in an attempt to reach the sock.

A funny story, yes, but one with a message of caution: people are constantly affecting the way animals use their energy. Our goal wasn't to tease but to gain experience and insight into our (or at least one) local fox. Still, I used it only that one time.

Exercises

○ Get into the habit of viewing the lives of wildlife through the lens of vulnerability. Observing wildlife in this way not only gives us an idea of how our ancestors sometimes saw the world but can also open up windows to experience predatory events.

○ Experiment with baiting in a natural area near your home. If you live near a forested area, set a variety of bait nearby and check back daily to see who has come by. If you reside in the suburbs, place a suet feeder in your backyard to draw in a variety of birds, including woodpeckers. If you live in a larger metropolitan area, take some seed to the local park and feed the squirrels (if allowed). Note the times of day (and year) that seem to prompt the greatest activity. Is your target animal most active at dawn and dusk, or does it prefer the heat of the midday sun? If your animal is nocturnal, can you use a trail camera to pinpoint a specific time of activity? Is your animal more active during periods of abundance or scarcity? Does the weather influence your animal's desire to feed?

○ Place yourself in the mindset of different animals while asking questions that pertain to environmental pressures and survival. Each organism possesses a unique skill set, and a number of factors influence its behavior. Track your observations in your nature journal, being sure to write down any questions or theories you might have. By adopting a less human-centric point of view, you will learn to think more like an animal and discover areas where you can potentially affect the behavior of an animal.

CHAPTER 8

Urban Wilderness and Backyard Awareness

Wilderness is not a luxury but a
necessity of the human spirit.

—EDWARD ABBEY

Years ago I worked at an after-school program in downtown Ithaca, New York. While outside on the playground one afternoon, I observed a pair of crows constructing a nest in one of the spruce trees at the edge of the schoolyard. Over the ensuing weeks I found great pleasure in watching the comings and goings of these urban corvids.

Eggs were laid and about eighteen days later they hatched. I vividly remember this day—there was clearly something different going on in the nest. Where once the patient mother sat, she now stood on the edge of the nest and looked in on her young hatchlings. There was much activity as the adults brought food home to their newborns. Eventually I began to see small black heads peering over the edge of the nest. One young bird was obviously the handful of the bunch. As this particular bird grew, I noticed she had trouble staying put; her parents often expressed concern as she explored the tree's dense branches.

One day I arrived at work surprised to see the new crows had been banded by a team of researchers from Cornell University's Lab of Ornithology. Owing to the new black wing tag adorned with white letters, the most mischievous of the fledglings now had a name: KT. She continued her antics, expanding her range from the nest into the spruce's environs.

On my walk to school one afternoon, I heard a spate of urgent distress calls. About a block from the school I located the adult crows. KT had apparently glided across the street, landed in a hedge between two houses, and caught the attention of a neighborhood cat. Although I rarely intrude on and disrupt the natural order, I had grown especially fond of this family and decided to come to KT's rescue. I chased off the cat and used a broom to persuade KT off the top of the hedge. She awkwardly landed in the middle of a driveway where I covered her with my flannel shirt.

While all this was happening I was being pursued and heckled by her parents; this mating pair and the previous year's offspring swept dangerously close to my head. Once captured, an ungrateful KT hissed at me. I quickly walked her across the street and into the schoolyard to the base of the spruce. I unwrapped the young crow from my flannel, held her aloft in my hands, and tossed her up into the tree.

KT found her way to the nest and became a model child. Her once cavalier personality was now cautious. She listened to her parents and went on to live the life of an urban crow. But after the incident with

PREVIOUS IMAGE Crows are excellent birds to observe. They are social, have an array of interesting behaviors to notice, and are never far from humans. (Kevin J. McGowan)

the cat, my presence was no longer tolerated. Crows perched near the school and heckled me. I even tried removing my hat and using a different door when leaving the building, but nothing worked. Eventually the young crows became strong enough to leave the nest. I would see KT around the neighborhood from time to time with her black wing tag with white letters.

This story and others like it illustrate the notion that you don't need to travel to grand, out-of-the-way places to commune with nature. Animals of all stripes—coyotes, falcons, raccoons, and such—appear to have found and capitalized on the innumerable resources available to them within the constructs of civilization. Just because your suburban or urban neighborhood is familiar doesn't mean it isn't replete with opportunities to view a wide variety of wildlife.

In my local county seat of Ithaca, New York, many unexpected wild animals either make their home in the shadows (and sometimes out of them) or pass through. I have spotted coyotes, foxes (both red and gray), and a myriad of migrating birds. In and around the waters of Stewart Park, which borders the city along the shores of Cayuga Lake, 270 bird species have been spotted! That works out to be about 33 percent of all birds species in the the entire country. Our urban creeks see runs of salmon, trout, and eels. Most recently, young sturgeon, which are being reestablished, have started to spawn up Fall Creek; they swim past the high school, the backyards of urban homes, and up to the base of massive Ithaca Falls, all within the city limits.

It's easy to pass through the world oblivious to your surroundings, be they wild or urban. Awareness, ultimately, is a choice. That isn't to say that the skills presented in this book don't require time to develop, but uniting with nature wherever it's found ultimately hinges on your desire to cultivate this way of experiencing the world.

Why Urban Wilderness and Why Now?

Urban wilderness is anything but urbane. Everything in these pages—the skills, approaches, and philosophies—is no less applicable to environments dominated by humanity than to wilderness. When I find

This young red fox was born within the confines of a city park in Ithaca, New York. The original den was hidden in a small patch of trees bounded with railroad tracks and an on-ramp on one side and a driveway within the park on the other. As the spring progressed and the kits got bigger, the mother moved the den a short distance away into the larger woods.

Nature Connections in Urban and Suburban Areas

More than a few excellent books encourage backyard, suburban, and urban nature restoration, participation, and connection, including these:

- *Attracting Birds, Butterflies, and Other Backyard Wildlife* by David Mizejewski
- *Hummingbird Gardens: Turning Your Yard into Hummingbird Heaven* by Stephen W. Kress
- *Nature Obscura* by Kelly Brenner
- *Rescuing the Planet* by Tony Hiss
- *Turning Homeward: Restoring Hope and Nature in the Urban Wild* by Adrienne Ross Scanlan
- *Welcome to Subirdia* by John Marzluff

Also, the USDA has excellent information on landscaping for wildlife at fs.fed.us/wildflowers/Native_Plant_Materials/Native_Gardening/landscapingforwildlife.shtml.

myself in urban and suburban areas, I am just as vigilant about detecting wildlife as I am in wilder places. In truth, a greater density of wildlife often exists closer to humanity than in truly feral ecosystems. As the global population expands and we continue to encroach on natural areas, the collision of these two seemingly incompatible worlds is inevitable.

A number of reasons account for the proliferation of wildlife in metropolitan areas. For one, if an animal can avoid being hit by an automobile, a city can serve as a safe haven from many predators. (This trend seems to be shifting as coyotes, foxes, and birds of prey are now adapting to take advantage of these situations.)

This fisher, photographed by a camera trap, has succeeded in killing a gray squirrel. (Melissa Groo)

In addition to unique opportunities to find food—in Dumpsters, garbage cans, and compost bins—urban centers offer animals safety from human hunting. Once species learn where these spaces are located, they may find life far less stressful than if they were to live in a heavily forested area. I know the deer in my rural locale are much more concerned with the comings and goings of humans than their suburban counterparts a mere fifteen miles away. There is something about the prospect of being shot that makes an animal hypervigilant.

Urban landscapes also offer an array of sheltering opportunities. Abandoned buildings and tunnels, sewer systems, and attics all offer places for sanctuary. When red-tailed hawks became comfortable nesting in Manhattan, one famous pair decided to build their home on a ledge near actress Mary Tyler Moore's apartment on Fifth Avenue. From their vantage atop this stately building, this pair of raptors was able to hunt for quarry in nearby Central Park.

When I visit the local big-box, do-it-yourself store, I often pause to admire the house sparrows that have taken up residence in the warehouselike structure. These resourceful birds have found almost everything they need here to live comfortably. As I listen, I hear territorial singing. I witness spats between rival males as they jockey over coveted perches and nesting spots. And I observe these birds scavenging. Inevitably, seed from some of the bags sold to backyard bird watchers is left behind, helping to make living inside a store a safe and worthwhile endeavor. While checking out one afternoon, I commented to the cashier about her feathered residents. I was amazed when she told me that the birds had learned to let themselves in and out of the store by fluttering in front of the electric eye that triggers the doors to open.

When choosing locations for settlements, humans tend to build in inviting locations such as valleys, ocean beaches, and lakesides rather than mountaintops, deserts, and other environments with comparatively lean resources. Places where people settle also tend to be warmer, and they are often next to waterways and waterfalls, which are attractive to wildlife. Being close to humanity can also offer animals a greater variety of plant life. In the Northeast, for example, forests once dominated the landscape, but now New England and the Mid-Atlantic states are a patchwork of timber, agriculture, and everything in between. These transition areas offer an array of resources to the enterprising forager (and, in turn, the enterprising predator).

Going beyond recognizing wildlife within an urban context to see how much you can learn about these unique adaptations will challenge and reward you. All of the requisite elements of behavior and survival are the same here as they are in the wilderness; in order to best understand how these needs are met within a manmade environment, it is again helpful to cast yourself in an animal-centric frame of mind.

Within that animal mindset, ask yourself the following questions: Where can I go to find shelter? How can I travel safely without being seen? Where can I find food? Regardless of the animal, certain needs must be met. The only distinction is that the opportunities and resources look different from those in wilder places. Golf courses, cemeteries, urban parks and waterways, urban greenways,

Eastern coyotes are an incredibly adaptable species and are found in virtually any kind of habitat. Besides living in wilder places, some eastern coyotes have made themselves at home within large cities such as Toronto, Canada. (Melissa Groo)

alleys, rooftops, and many other locations can offer favorable circumstances for wildlife. I once stepped outside of an outdoor gear store in a strip mall to take a call from a good friend. As we caught up, I noticed a Cooper's hawk glide over the top of a big-box store and ambush a pigeon. I gasped at the intense moment. This hawk clearly knew what it was doing and was able to feed itself with minimal effort.

Historical Changes: Two Examples

The last two centuries have seen remarkable changes in habitat that speak to the impact humans have had on the environment and native species. In many parts of the Northeast, areas that were once clear-cut to support agricultural production have since been reclaimed by forests. Two animals come to mind that epitomize the consequences of unfettered land use coupled with ill-conceived wildlife management practices: the white-tailed deer and the eastern coyote.

As Indigenous peoples were driven westward and/or forced onto reservations during colonial expansion and Europeans began claiming the land, predatory species came to be seen as a threat to livestock. One species that was eliminated from much of its range was the

Urban Considerations

Crossing paths with urban wildlife brings with it the same responsibility as experiencing wildlife anywhere, with the understanding that animals in urban areas may have less cover to retreat to. Be respectful, courteous, and mindful of how your presence is affecting the animal you are close to. It is very likely that any suburban and urban animals or birds you encounter will be somewhat habituated to the presence of people. Generally, the baseline of comfort for wild residents in the city is very different from what it is in their more rural or wild environments. This comparative comfort with people can lend itself well to some excellent viewing opportunities. Still, do your best not to get too close and pressure animals, which could make them flee into traffic or stress them in other ways.

eastern wolf. As the result of persecution through hunting and poisoning, this large canine was relegated to the Canadian wilderness.

In time, the modest agricultural operations of the Northeast were replaced by large-scale farming enterprises on midwestern plateaus, where they were more practical. These changes meant that much of the open space used for farming was left fallow, and nature soon took over. These overgrown fields turned into thicket and immature forests—a perfect habitat for deer.

When I was a child, I witnessed the explosion in deer population firsthand. I often wandered the woodlot and fields near my home in suburban Buffalo. In the beginning, I would see only hawks, owls, and foxes, but deer were a novelty seen when we went camping in the country. I remember the day my friend Don and I spotted a trio of deer across a field that bordered a large creek. We were excited about these new arrivals, but within a few short years the population had increased exponentially.

White-tailed deer went from a fleeting rarity to being so numerous that you couldn't help spotting them as they burst forth from their neighborhood strongholds. On one particular evening, I counted *more than two hundred* between a large field and a neighboring golf course. This explosion of white-tails seemed to happen overnight. With ideal habitat, no hunting, and no natural predators, their proliferation soon became an issue.

But while deer populations were on the rise, another amazing development was under way. A new species—the coywolf or eastern coyote—was increasing in numbers and finding new turf. Filling the void left by the elimination of the eastern wolf, western coyotes moved into new territories and spread northward. These wayfarers eventually found their way into Algonquin Provincial Park in Ontario, Canada.

The native eastern wolves, whose numbers were depleted, leapt at the opportunity to breed with these new residents, and hybridization took place. The coywolf, or eastern coyote, is essentially a western coyote on steroids; it is larger than its western kin, with longer legs and more powerful jaws. Most important, this animal has multiplied throughout the Northeast, spreading not only into wild places but also into true "urban jungles."

Eastern coyotes have now set up shop in large metropolitan areas including Toronto and New York City. With deer numbers at an all-time high (and with little competition), the Northeast has become a home for this newer, effective predator. Unlike the western coyote, which prefers to hunt small game, the eastern coyote is capable of tackling larger quarry and has even been known to bring down elk and moose. *Meet the Coywolf* is an excellent PBS documentary detailing this phenomenon.

Backyard Awareness

A multitude of simple methods can be used to coax wildlife into the open by providing the elements they require for survival. This leads us to a discussion of what I've dubbed backyard awareness.

I find backyard awareness to be one of life's great pleasures. Few things are as thrilling as glancing out my window from the comfort of my kitchen to catch a glimpse of a unique or interesting visitor. Installing

I discovered this coal skink in my driveway. It was the only time I have seen one of these elusive reptiles.

bird feeders, bird baths, and bat houses and planting fruiting shrubs (as well as making other habitat improvements, including growing butterfly host plants) can make even the most seemingly inhospitable environment suddenly inviting. To me making our homes welcoming to butterflies and other wildlife is among the easiest ways to not only do something positive for our wild kin but also enrich our own lives.

In our yard, we have planted flowers that support our growing ruby-throated hummingbird population. The flowers along with two feeders make them a constant and entertaining presence. They have become comfortable to the point of sitting on our fingers as they take nectar from the feeder held in our hands. Garter snakes seem to be multiplying each year as well. Gardens, rock walls, and scrap piles of wood put out intentionally have made superb habitat for these beautiful reptiles.

On a visit to the Buffalo area, I met up with my old friend Don, who had recently purchased a house in an older neighborhood in Williamsville, New York. Don has been interested in connecting with nature for as long as I've known him. He had planted a variety of fruit trees and berry bushes and also set up a bird feeder. Despite living in an environment where humans are a dominant presence, Don shares his backyard with white-tailed deer, eastern cottontails, nesting robins, and foxes.

A mile or so away we fished the local creek. This wild corridor within the boundaries of the village of Williamsville held sign of beaver, mink, and raccoon. We also saw steelhead trout that had migrated from the Niagara River. As we fished we observed turkey vultures, mallards, and a belted kingfisher surveying the banks.

As much as backyard awareness is an intentional process, sometimes discovery is the result of dumb luck. One summer I was mowing the grass in my front yard when I saw something odd shuffle through the gravel on my driveway. I hopped off the lawnmower to get a closer look. To my astonishment, it was one of the most elusive lizards in all of New York State—the coal skink. Many naturalists go a lifetime without seeing one in its natural habitat (this was the first time I had ever seen one myself), and here was a healthy juvenile basking in plain sight! Its reptilian skin shone with brilliance. Occurring only in isolated populations, these lizards are surprisingly quick. I gently crept toward it, instructed my son Jacob to grab the camera, and snapped a photograph before it disappeared.

Exercises

- Identify places where urban wildlife can be found. Look for signs of activity, and track identified animals to see how and where they get their needs met. Wherever you find yourself, don't forget to use the skills presented in this book.

- Being mindful of safety, try to experience the urban wilderness at all times of day as well as during all types of weather.

- Encourage wildlife to see your backyard as a refuge. Provide bird feeders, housing, and habitat and grow beneficial plants.

CHAPTER 9

Spontaneous Acceptance

All who are in touch with the natural
world can sense energies, emotions, and
intentions of people and animals. If we
listen, we can know. All we need to do is
give up being in charge. Knowing inside is
not something unusual; it is how we are.
All humans can have that connection with
All-That-Is. The connection is within us.

—ROBERT WOLFF, *ORIGINAL WISDOM: STORIES OF AN
ANCIENT WAY OF KNOWING*

In my early twenties I worked as the assistant director at an
environmental education center in the Berkshire Mountains of
Massachusetts. Although I loved my job, I found it difficult to carve
out time to be by myself. I enjoyed my time alone and felt it was never
quite enough.

At the conclusion of our summer session, we were given a week
off before preparing for the fall term. Without hesitation I packed

my car, loaded my kayak, and headed to Ontario for a seven-day paddling trip.

I arrived at my favorite launch point with no expectations regarding what I would do or where I would go. After checking in with the forest ranger, I packed my vessel and headed off onto Canoe Lake. I ventured out at a leisurely pace that enabled me to soak in the beauty of my surroundings. At the end of the lake I made a short carry into a more remote body of water and found myself drifting aimlessly with the wind. I felt calm and grateful and more at peace than I had in some time.

As I floated along, a loon emerged from the water not ten feet from my boat. I figured it hadn't noticed me because I was idle and that it was a coincidence that it had surfaced so nearby. I expected it to startle and disappear. To my astonishment, the loon held its position and regarded me with an air of curiosity. Instead of dipping into the water, it floated along with me for several minutes, even calling at one point. I was in awe. The loon left me as I drifted into the shallows at the end of the lake.

I made my way up a small creek toward the next portage. As I came around a bend, I noticed ripples coming from the side of the bank. I drew closer and saw a beaver sitting at the water's edge. He tensed for a moment, but instead of fleeing he looked at me, picked up a small branch, and calmly resumed chewing. I watched this semi-aquatic rodent for a few moments and then continued on my way.

I soon found myself on Burnt Island Lake, a large backcountry reservoir with numerous bays and islands, and established camp near the ruins of a historic resort. As I set up my tarp, a large bird glided through the trees and landed on the ground at the edge of my camp. It was a raven. I continued to work, moving in a calm fashion but taking no particular action to conceal my presence.

PREVIOUS IMAGE With males and females both well camouflaged for their habitat, ruffed grouse are more often heard than seen when the males drum. As they beat their wings against themselves they create a noise that sounds a bit like a lawnmower starting up. (iStock/photobirder)

This normally wary bird sat and observed me as I worked. I have seen many ravens, but it was a new experience to have one sitting so contentedly in my presence. After dinner I hung up my bear bag and decided to wander around to see if I could find any evidence of the once-popular resort that had stood nearby. I found glass jars, an old foundation, and an assortment of iron scrap. I even followed a ruffed grouse as I made my way through the brush; I moved slowly enough that it didn't startle and fly away.

My close encounters with wildlife continued over the ensuing days. I saw innumerable otters and was able to float in my kayak and watch them forage in a small bay. One even emerged from the water with a sunfish in its jaws and then consumed it on the beach. These animals are a true joy to behold, one of a few species to regularly play as adults. On another small creek that was perhaps a dozen feet wide, a great blue heron allowed me to paddle past without showing any signs of alarm.

Though I had been observing wildlife for years, what happened over the course of these few days was new and unprecedented. Animals not only seemed calm in my presence but also appeared to mirror my inquisitiveness. There was nothing in their body language to indicate that I was perceived as a threat.

That changed about halfway through the week. Up until that point, I was meandering at a pace that felt comfortable. I was free to poke around in my kayak and wander through the forest without concern for time. At the midpoint of my journey, however, I realized I had put myself so deep into Algonquin Provincial Park that I would need to paddle hard to ensure I returned to Massachusetts in time for the start of fall term.

My magical encounters with wildlife came to an abrupt end. Any animals I came upon were seen fleeing or heard crashing through the brush. Moose are often leisurely in their encounters with humans, but the one I saw that week fled as if it were being pursued by a pack of hungry wolves. It was the only moose out of hundreds I have encountered that I have ever seen running. What had changed, ultimately, was my body language and state of mind. I was hurried. I had an agenda. And I had surrendered the possibility of wandering for the obligation of getting back to my car and my job.

The Most Fundamental Skills

The information in this chapter exists on its own plane and represents an unequivocal departure from everything that has come before. Of all the skills associated with observing wildlife, those that result in what I call spontaneous acceptance of your presence by animals are by far the most difficult to define and develop. Up to this point, I have touted invisibility as the most fundamental and vital skill—it establishes the foundation for positioning oneself to witness, approach, learn from, and manipulate wildlife.

But one's ability to successfully infiltrate the matrix of the wild also relies on a willingness to accept whatever might come without the least bit of pretense or attention to time. The idea of going without time or letting go of being in charge as Robert Wolff suggests may seem odd or foreign. Still, one of the greatest gifts we can give ourselves is to allow time away from the modern world to truly unwind in the wilderness and trust that we will know what we need to know when we need to know it.

I wish I could say I am in touch with this energy all of the time. I am not. It seems that the pressures and goals of the modern world conflict with this way of being. When I have experienced this deep and profound way of knowing, though, it is as natural as anything; synchronicities happen and intuition is as easy to interpret as words on a page. I have gotten into this mental state on wilderness excursions when I have let go of agenda and expectation and have opened myself to be guided by a greater force, but that is a story for another day.

The following philosophies can be used in conjunction with (and sometimes in spite of) the wisdom I have attempted to share in the previous chapters. But you can't force these approaches to experiencing wildlife. Those that result in spontaneous acceptance are the most intuitive of skills; the most I can say is, when the time is right, you'll know.

As I see it, there are two main skills that you can use either in combination with or independent from each other. The first, the notion of intentional body language, relies on an acute awareness of how animals respond to your presence. The second requires an internal state of calm—what is sometimes known as the quiet mind. This enables wildlife to accept and relate to you as a benign, nonthreatening entity.

Intentional Body Language

Using intentional body language can help you not only in entering the forest but also in recovering should you become exposed. (If you've been busted, acting in an indifferent and nonthreatening way can sometimes put animals at ease and allow you to continue observing them.) Intentional body language is especially useful if you're attempting to build a relationship with an animal and want to demonstrate that you are a benevolent force.

It's important to remember your intent must be genuine. If you attempt to employ these skills but are insincere in your intention, meaning you have ulterior motives that may bring harm, animals will undoubtedly distrust you and move away. Remember, animals have senses that are far more refined than ours, as well as senses we don't have, and all have been shaped by evolution to promote their survival. The purpose of displaying intentional body language is to show that you have no vested interest in your quarry and are essentially harmless.

Much like when you're learning to stealth walk and move through the landscape, your success will be determined largely by the way the animals in your proximity respond. The difference between intentional body language and invisibility is that with the former you know you're being watched by the animals around you and your intent is to put them at ease with your actions and movement.

When I discussed this philosophy with veteran Primitive Pursuits instructor Sean Cornell, he told me of a recent experiment he'd conducted with body language. On solo excursions into a local forest, Sean had modified his gait to move slowly and with extreme caution. He noted that the animals in his environs appeared to accept his presence more willingly when he moved in this way. They did not perceive him as a threat. By way of comparison, when Sean moved with greater exuberance, the wildlife around him became increasingly vigilant.

Several autumns ago I was spending much of my free time on a wooded hillside that borders the affluent neighborhood of Cayuga

Heights near Ithaca, New York. Despite the forest's proximity to a highly populated locale, it was replete with wildlife—I saw turkeys, squirrels, hawks, foxes, and deer. This particular season I was following HO2, the large ten-point buck I mentioned in Chapter 3.

Over a period of weeks I came close to being able to predict where I would find him. One day, after scouring the woods for close to an hour, I decided to move to where the scrub at the top of the hill met a neighborhood backyard. I saw an antler move behind a pile of downed timber, and using natural cover I inched closer. I soon found myself less than thirty yards away from HO2. I sat for a while, enjoying the company of this magnificent ungulate as he lay resting in a pool of sunlight.

I decided to slowly stand up and move into the open so he could see me. Although HO2 was a suburban white-tail and familiar with the comings and goings of humanity, my behavior was in contrast with his normal baseline. I have visited these woods many times and have never seen another person. I was turned to the side, facing away from him and slowly moving away as if unaware of his presence. I acted as if I were grazing. I stopped to fiddle with a twig and otherwise tried to indicate that I had my mind on other things.

Over time I indirectly moved closer, mindful of HO2's comfort. I walked slowly but was well aware that I was being watched. At no point did he indicate alarm. I eventually took a seat on a log not twenty feet away. Even if you choose to use body language to approach an animal as I did in this instance, remember to be cautious. Don't get close—in the ways I am suggesting in this section—to animals that have the potential to harm you. Remember the safety considerations discussed in Chapter 1 at all times. Also keep these pointers in mind:

- **Try for an honest expression of calm, friendly, and even joyful feelings.** Animals can sense ill intent regardless of how slow or quiet your movements may be. Stay attuned to how your movements and actions will be perceived.
- **Maintain an animal-centric point of view.** You may even want to squat on the ground to invoke a nonthreatening posture. If you are moving too quickly or heading directly toward an animal,

for example, you may be perceived as aggressive. Being loud or moving excessively could also scare away animals. Learn from your experience. The animals will show you the way.

- **Let the animals around you know you're there.** (This point stands in stark contrast to the notion of invisibility.) Quietly vocalize and use gentle, easy movements so they can recognize your presence.
- **Pretend you're grazing, or examine a stone, feather, or leaf.** Work on a quiet craft that demonstrates you're engrossed in things that have nothing to do with the animal you've pursued; weave, carve, or make cordage.

In the summer of 2017 I was on an Adirondack camping trip with one of my youth groups. We were car camping near a small one-lane bridge that allowed the dirt road to pass over a beautiful little creek. The banks of the creek had been reinforced on either side of the bridge with large rocks to help prevent erosion. From the bridge we spotted about seven nice-sized garter snakes sunning themselves on the warmth of the stone. One of the girls with me, Brianna, wanted to catch a snake, as kids like to do. Instead, I encouraged her to move quietly down to the rocks and see if she could make friends.

Moving slowly below the bridge, she quietly made her way to a comfortable spot on the rocks near where the snakes had been hanging out. I gently coached her as she moved. She lay her hand down on one of the favorite spots. In short order two garters emerged from the cracks. One of them slithered up next to my young friend's hand and rested its head between her thumb and first finger. At this point it would be easy to think that the snake was unaware that a human was present.

As the snake rested, a second girl, Kelley, gently approached. By the time the second camper moved into place, Brianna was petting the snake with her index finger. After Kelley got situated, she also petted the snake, using her whole hand. The two snakes were not fazed in the least. If I were to guess, this was a first for these animals, and they seemed perfectly fine. The snakes eventually moved away, as Brianna had a hard time resisting the urge to try to hold one of them.

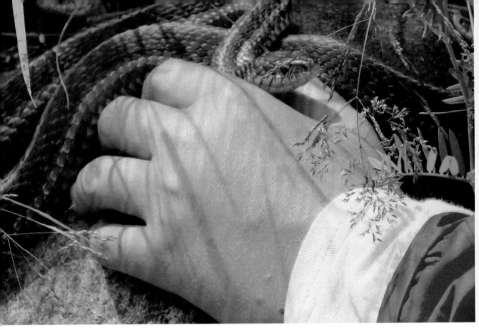

This garter snake came out from where it was hiding and ended up resting on the hand of a participant in my program. The snake remained there for a while, even as it was being petted.

The Quiet Mind

The emotional energy you exude has a direct bearing on your environment and how animals respond to your presence. The vast majority of human beings seem to have lost touch with a calm way of relating to nature; the stresses and expectations of the modern world do little to nurture the quiet mind.

The state of being that most adults (and young people) operate in within today's world is far different from that of our ancestors, who were intimately joined to nature's rhythms. Where once an awareness and knowledge of the land was essential, our minds are now driven largely by other motivations—economic, material, technological. This newer paradigm demands that we give our attention to being efficient, productive, and fast. Additionally, many other unnatural expectations take our attention away from nature and contribute to mental health issues and a harried mind.

I believe one of the most important things we can do to ensure our well-being is to take deliberate steps to cultivate a calm and open mind. That's crucial to putting the skills in this book into practice. When you are walking through the woods, I would encourage you to unplug from civilization. Because of the ubiquity of mobile devices, this is more difficult than you might think. But doing so enables you to truly leave the cares of the modern world and society in the rearview mirror. And this, my friends, is vital.

In my own experience, I know when I've reached a place where my mind is quiet when I've allowed myself to slow down. My internal chatter has dissipated, and I feel at peace with my surroundings. The behavior of the animals around me is a barometer of my internal calm and often mirrors this state of mind. I give myself the time and permission to unwind, to wander, to open up my senses, and just *be*. With enough time, a gentle focusing of my awareness helps lead me to this place.

Being accepted by virtue of a calm or quiet mind—spontaneous acceptance—although elusive, is indeed palpable. Many of my colleagues and I have had experiences with wildlife that seem to defy logic and are rooted more in energy and attitudes than quantifiable skills. Again, it is important to remember the governing tenets of this philosophy:

- Give yourself the gift of time devoted to enjoying life and nature.
- Abandon schedule, time, pretense, and expectations.
- Quiet yourself—both mind and body. (Review the "How to Be Still" sidebar in Chapter 2 for suggestions.)
- Meditate in a way that works for you. Focusing on the present moment can quiet the mind.
- Try to identify what is distracting you, acknowledge it, and let it go.
- Be willing to spend time alone and wander.
- Trust that you will be led along the right path. Allow yourself the space to meander.

My experiences and the experiences of others would seem to indicate that meaningful connection with wildlife is awarded to those who are open to new encounters and grateful for whatever comes their way.

A quality relationship with nature is often a reflection of your inner state. If you approach your wilderness experiences with an open mind and give yourself the time and permission to slow down, you will be rewarded with unique and special moments.

Still, I'm hesitant to make broad proclamations about what is, at its essence, a mysterious practice. Though I've had many unique experiences with wildlife, there is no set protocol. The common factors seem to have more to do with a mindset that is difficult to characterize until you get there. The people in my life who have regular encounters of this type are generally calm; they move quietly through the world and tend to be excellent observers. They are joyous when they have encounters with animals and are very thankful for the experiences they have had. Fortunately for those of us who don't have these qualities naturally, they can be learned and practiced.

On rare occasions I have had the honor of meeting people who seem to have that special, indescribable *something*. They intuitively possess the skills to incite close encounters with wildlife. Lily Glidden was one of those people. Lily once told me a story about a coyote she'd encountered in a patch of state forest near her home. This typically retiring and cautious mammal displayed no signs of apprehension. Instead, it maintained a comfortable distance and exhibited an air of curiosity, even choosing to follow her down the trail for a while. Lily had that gift of attracting animals. They were unthreatened and comfortable in her presence. She had a peaceful and easygoing way when she moved through the land. Additionally, she was one of the most joyous and grateful people I have ever had the honor of knowing.

My good friend Eryn relayed a story to me along similar lines. As a researcher at Hubbard Brook Experimental Forest in New Hampshire, Eryn was tasked with discovering and monitoring black-throated blue warbler nests. This job, which Eryn is naturally gifted for, requires you to be incredibly aware and calm, and to move with great care. As Eryn was looking quietly into the branches of a hobblebush, a shrub preferred by the warblers to nest in, she was startled to notice a white-tailed doe not ten feet away. Eryn said, "Hi there." The deer

Black-throated blue warblers love the shady forest understory, nesting in the mixed wood-lands of the Northeast. (iStock/BrianLasenby)

clearly knew Eryn was present yet showed no sign of alarm and seemed interested in staying near her as she quietly went about her research.

Eryn reiterated to me the importance of being calm and paying attention as a field biologist. To discover black-throated blue warbler nests, she first hears and spots a male singing. When the male changes his song to a "whisper" or softer song, she knows that the female is close by. The females are difficult to spot and only chip softly, so patience and attentiveness are required to see them. When they are building their nests, the females hop around the forest with the male in tow, collecting materials such as bark and spiderwebs. If they feel comfortable enough with your presence, they will go down to their nests and add the pieces they have collected. Eryn feels it is a great privilege to experience this window into these birds' lives, achieved simply with mindfulness and careful observation.

Being accepted by an animal or a group of animals yields some truly wonderful benefits. At best, it establishes a new baseline. While a human presence often equates to an environmental disturbance, being accepted into the tribe of the wild reinforces the notion that you are *of the forest*—a perspective that will pay dividends. Animals inevitably take cues from one another and will be much more likely to act within baseline behaviors that include you if you've taken the time to fully integrate into your surroundings.

My year with Merle the beaver allowed me to put to use all of the skills I've outlined in this book. Merle arrived at our small pond most likely after plodding up the small stream that leads to the substantial creek in the valley at the bottom of our hill. At the very least, he traveled unprotected for more than a mile. Our pond, as small as it is, offered deep water for protection. On Merle's first evening with us, I crept to the edge of the pond. Trying to be as nonthreatening as possible, I just sat. This routine, coupled with apple slices tossed into the water, was met with only a few tail slaps. (I was inspired by Dorothy Richards's book *Beaversprite* and made a deliberate choice to feed Merle. Inadvertent or intentional feeding isn't recommended for some animals, such as black bears, who will feed on rural and suburban garbage or other foods left outside and then become sufficiently habituated to view humans too closely.)

Within three days, Merle was collecting apples and grooming on the shore near my position. In a short time he grew to recognize my voice and understand that I was coming down the trail. He'd swim my way when he heard me ask, "Who's a beaver?" Merle became so comfortable with my presence that he would often sit less than ten feet from me with his back turned toward me as he went through his maintenance routine.

To gain access to a front-row seat to a wild animal's life, much like Jane Goodall did with gorillas and Joe Hutto did with wild turkeys, is humbling, life changing, and incredibly informative. Aside from some days away from home and a period of six weeks when ice covered our pond, I sat every evening to witness the life of a bachelor beaver. I became part of Merle's normal, and he became part of mine. I was witness to his daily activities, heard many vocalizations, experienced his reactions to threats, and saw him foraging for ferns, grasses, and clover. Once my son Jacob and I saw him eat a snail.

Merle became used to my daily visits and would approach the pond edge where I would sit after I quietly called, "Who's a beaver?" I became part of his baseline, part of his normal surroundings.

I often noticed that waterfowl frequenting the pond seemed to possess a greater capacity for tolerating my presence than I might have otherwise anticipated. On one occasion a pair of wood ducks, which are typically skittish, lingered near the pond's edge and then casually waddled up into the forest. The beaver didn't care that I was there, so why should they?

Yet Merle wasn't habituated to all humans, just the ones close to him whom he trusted and chose to include in his baseline. He retained his wariness toward other humans. When my friend, photographer Melissa Groo, came to take pictures of Merle, he'd have nothing to do with her despite her being still, quiet, and patient.

I am convinced that Indigenous people around the globe have had relationships of this sort with wildlife since the beginning of time. Animals hold a wisdom that transcends our daily concerns and can teach us in unique and meaningful ways. Merle taught me how to move and how not to be too still, and he allowed me to observe the comings and goings of his life for more than a year. Now that Merle has moved on, I have dreamt of him swimming with other beavers in some not-too-distant wetland.

Another example is told in the PBS documentary *My Life as a Turkey*, where biologist Joe Hutto gains access to the rich and complicated lives of wild turkeys. Through an intimate understanding of vocalizations and body language, Hutto heightens his awareness so that he is eventually coached by his feathered kin to see potential threats, including eastern diamondback rattlesnakes, lurking in the Florida flatlands.

Be open to the possibilities of not just observing wildlife but also becoming part of their normal. It is hard to express how beautiful and powerful these kinds of relationships can be.

Exercises

- Practice quiet movement with the understanding (and expectation) that you will be detected by area wildlife. Periodically recalibrate your state of mind (you'll be amazed at how often you need to do this) and take stock of how animals respond to your presence. Make note of the results and adjust your approaches accordingly.

- Mindful movement is an important component of facilitating access to the quiet mind. If you experience difficulty silencing internal chatter, stealth walking while using owl eyes (see Chapter 3) can work as a means of meditation. I personally find canoeing a relaxing and contemplative activity. Being on the water allows for a different perspective and often rewards the naturalist with great recompense. Repetitive activities such as working with your hands are also an effective way of focusing and quieting the mind. Experiment.

- As animals begin to accept your presence, take stock of how your addition to the landscape impacts the environment's baseline. Grant special consideration to the animals you are close to so you can learn from their specific skill sets.

CHAPTER 10

Reconnecting with Nature

Change is never easy, and it often creates discord, but when people come together for the good of humanity and the Earth, we can accomplish great things.

—DAVID SUZUKI

I n Southeast Asia lives a tribe of Indigenous peoples known as the Moken. The Moken are a loosely knit group of nomads whose home is found near the waters of the Andaman Sea. Subsisting on what they harvest from the ocean, the Moken are a highly observant band of people. Their lives are intimately tied to nature's rhythms, to the fish, birds, and other animals that live along and near the coast. Their deep knowledge of the environment provides the Moken with everything they need to survive.

Like all peoples, the Moken have legends. One such legend speaks of the Seven Waves and the Angry Sea. This tale has been passed down from generation to generation, and it carries clues to the Mokens' survival. The story describes how during the period known as the Seven

Waves, the tide moved out farther than normal, dolphins swam out to sea, and animals that made their home near the coast sought higher ground. These signs indicated the approach of a tsunami, a rare seismic event that is difficult, if not impossible, to predict.

On December 26, 2004, the Moken observed this legend come to life. Those residing in coastal villages took to the hills. Those on the water headed out to sea. The clues from nature were available for anyone to observe but were noted and taken seriously only by the Moken. More than 230,000 people died on that tragic day in Southeast Asia as a result of the Sumatra-Andaman Earthquake. But no Moken lives were lost, thanks to the culture's stories and values that encouraged its members to pay attention to nature and its inhabitants, and to take life-saving action.

It is my hope that this book guides readers in forging deeper and more meaningful relationships with wildlife and the natural world. Our humanness traditionally has been defined by our affinity for the earth, which includes a purposeful connection with the plants and animals that inhabit it. But what was once the norm has since been replaced with a paradigm of disconnection and indifference. In contemporary society, where spending time outside is often treated like a novelty, the value of slowing down and connecting with nature cannot be overstated.

The fact we've become so disconnected from Earth's rhythms that we now have to make a determined effort to encourage people of all ages to get outdoors is lamentable. But it is still worth making the effort. There is an increasing need to advocate for and protect wildlife, as much for the health of our ecosystem as for the health of future generations.

The changes humanity has inflicted upon the environment are almost beyond comprehension. As the Industrial Revolution gathered momentum and morphed into the modern technological age, our

---

PREVIOUS SPREAD Marmots are alpine residents that are commonly seen as well as heard; they emit a shrill whistle in response to perceived danger. (iStock/KenCanning)

influence gained increased traction. With each innovation, rarely have we paused to consider the long-term repercussions. As we move forward in the name of progress, I believe it is imperative that we ask, To what end? What will our legacy become? I often wonder if the issues of our times are unique to the human experience or more likely symptoms of a species out of balance with its environment. Our survival hinges on asking such questions.

The Presence of Humanity and the Modern Dilemma

Modern humanity is beset with an inescapable dilemma: within the construct of our never-ending desire for "progress," we have placed ourselves at odds with the natural world. Like a virus, we have proliferated and mutated the methods through which we manipulate the earth, our host, to meet our needs.

Across the United States, clear-cutting and deforestation have led to the destruction of native habitats. The use of coal and our dependence on oil are now being replaced with "clean" energy in the form of natural gas, the extraction of which, from underground shale formations, is threatening the purity of our water. As the global population continues to swell, more demands will ultimately be placed on our planet. Without a clear vision of the legacy we hope to impart to future generations, the outcome may indeed be dire.

It's easy to dismiss the idea of extinction, for example, as something confined to more distant and uninformed times; the eastern elk (1887), Southern California kit fox (1903), and passenger pigeon (1914) all disappeared from our earth more than a century ago. But numerous species have succumbed to extinction in just the last ten years, including the West African black rhino, the Yangtze River dolphin, and the Japanese river otter.

A 2017 article in the *Guardian* about a conference at the Vatican on biological extinction reported on this dilemma: "One in five species on Earth now faces extinction, and that will rise to 50% by the end of the century unless urgent action is taken. That is the stark view of the world's leading biologists, ecologists and economists."

Adapting to or letting go of modern conveniences while maintaining an intimate connection with ancestral practices is the challenge we now face. As noted psychologist Carl Jung wrote, "Something in man is profoundly disinclined to give up his beginnings." We require a new approach—one predicated not on dependence or estrangement, but *interdependence*. And this notion of interdependence—and hope—surfaces time and again in the literature. Only by embracing our past connection as one species among many connected to nature will we find hope for a future for all species.

Where Do We Go from Here?

I remember the first time I caught a fish with my hands. It was early spring, and with wet feet I crouched in the shallow waters of a modest creek that ran through an urban neighborhood. Despite my setting, I was essentially a premodern person waiting with a hunter's stillness for my quarry to swim past. I positioned my hands in a spot where the fish were sure to funnel through and, after catching hold of one, clumsily flung it onto the rocks at just the right moment. But over time, my technique improved; the fish taught me to move slowly, and I became skilled at lifting them from the water with less splash, more poetry.

If you haven't figured it out yet, this book is essentially about hunting the way our forebearers did—yet it's now more a seeking of connection. No gadgets or gizmos, just an intimate and honest use of your senses, coupled with targeted questions and the ability to learn. How you choose to use these skills is up to you. Hunting for connection is as important in our time as hunting for subsistence was in theirs. Be respectful, humble, and open to whatever drama nature grants you. Your version of hunting might not involve the harvesting of an animal but instead a photograph, a memory, or a simple yet important experience. All of these can help foster your connection to your place.

Above all else, remain open to whatever nature presents to you. Understanding and connecting with wildlife isn't a prize to be won or treasure to be found. It's already a part of you just waiting to be awakened and revived.

Exercises

○ Combine your newfound observational skills with a local citizen science project. A great place to start could be CitSci (citsci.org), or SciStarter (scistarter.org), or the Great Backyard Bird Count (birdcount.org).

○ Learn about habitats and animals' survival needs by helping replant forests or participating in other habitat restoration. Returning to a habitat for ongoing restoration work is a great way to learn how wildlife uses a place over time.

○ Create a backyard wildlife sanctuary.

○ Go on family-oriented nature explorations so parents and children can learn together.

ACKNOWLEDGMENTS

I am so thankful to the many people who have shared my enthusiasm for wildlife. I have been blessed by their support and inspiration in the creation of this book.

Thank you to one of my oldest and dearest friends, Don Vizzi. Don's drive to get outside and immerse himself in the wilds of New York State is still as contagious today as it was when we were kids. Love you, Bait!

Over the past twenty-five years, I've been honored to work with countless amazing young people through my employment with Cornell Cooperative Extension 4H in Tompkins County, New York. A special thank you to Brianna, Kelley, Kaylie, Frank, Morgan, Angus, and Lily. A special note of gratitude to my friend Eryn Woernley, who at the age of thirteen was entrusted with an early version of this manuscript and gave it her approval.

I have had the privilege of working with a most amazing team of naturalists through the Primitive Pursuits program. This includes Jed Jordan, Tim Drake, Sean Cornell, Justin Sutera, Heidi Bardy, Jeremiah Aviel, Lauren Salzman, and Sarah Chaffee.

Deep appreciation for Laura Ryan's graceful cleanup of my chicken scratch. She made me appear to be a better writer than I actually am.

Thank you to Melissa Groo for connecting me to Mountaineers Books as well as for contributing some of her stunning photographs.

I am grateful to many friends who share my enthusiasm for spending time in wild places. These people include Andy Zepp, Megan Ludgate, Connor Roberson, Elliott Swarthout, Beth Bannister, and Shelley Lester.

A special thank-you to Dave Muska, who is always willing to go winter camping and tracking with me when no one else will.

Thank you to Kevin McGowan for providing a wonderful photo as well as for refreshing my memory about the details of the wing tag on KT, the urban crow.

Thanks to Jason Hamilton for his generosity in letting me use and adapt his track chart. Additional thanks for his willingness to share his incredible knowledge of tracking and the excellent discussion regarding the lack of consensus about terminology among professionals. And thank you to Gary Schober for his professional advice.

When I was a young person, my parents provided me with many opportunities that helped foster a love of all things wild through our treks to the Adirondacks, Maine, Letchworth State Park, Cape Cod, and beyond. Thank you for your ongoing love and support.

Thank you to my favorite sister, Kate Russel (Pookie), my personal IT department.

Everyone associated with Mountaineers Books has been truly amazing to work with. So much appreciation for Kate Rogers, Adrienne Ross Scanlan, Janet Kimball, Lorraine Anderson, Patrick Barber, and Joeth Zucco.

I would like to express my love and gratitude to my wife, Sharon, and our sons, Jacob and Aron, for all their support and acceptance of my wild obsessions.

Finally, I would like to thank Merle, the beaver, and the countless wild creatures that have been a part of my life. They are the inspiration for this book.

PREVIOUS IMAGE Prairie dogs live in grasslands throughout the Great Plains region. (iStock/robertcicchetti)

SOURCES AND RESOURCES

In addition to the books and resources I've recommended throughout the text, here are some more resources to explore.

"Audubon's Guide to Ethical Bird Photography and Videography," audubon.org/get-outside/audubons-guide-ethical-bird-photography.

Dunne, Pete. *The Art of Pishing: How to Attract Birds by Mimicking Their Calls.* Mechanicsburg, PA: Stackpole Books, 2006. Includes audio CD.

Erickson, Dan. "7 Ways to Return to the Lost Art of Being Still," Hip Diggs, August 18, 2016, hipdiggs.com/being-still/.

Hall, Dave, with Jon Ulrich. *Winter in the Wilderness: A Field Guide to Primitive Survival Skills.* Ithaca, NY: Cornell University Press, 2015.

Laws, John Muir. *The Laws Guide to Nature Drawing and Journaling.* Berkeley, CA: Heyday, 2016.

McKie, Robin. "Biologists Think 50% of Species Will Be Facing Extinction by the End of the Century," *Guardian*, Feburary 25, 2017.

Nature: A Murder of Crows, directed by Susan Fleming. PBS DVD, 2011.

Nature: Meet the Coywolf, directed by Susan Fleming. PBS DVD, 2014.

Nature: My Life as a Turkey, directed by Fred Kaufman. PBS DVD, 2011.

Richards, Dorothy, with Hope Sawyer Buyukmihci. *Beaversprite: My Years Building an Animal Sanctuary.* Interlaken, NY: Heart of the Lakes Publishing, 1983.

Starnater, Eddie. *Principles of Natural Camouflage: The Science of Invisibility.* DVD, 2012.

———. *Principles of Natural Camouflage: The Art of Invisibility*, 2nd edition. Great Meadows, NJ: Feral Human Publications, 2015.

Wolff, Robert. *Original Wisdom: Stories of an Ancient Way of Knowing.* Rochester, VT: Inner Traditions, 2001.

Young, Jon. *What the Robin Knows: How Birds Reveal the Secrets of the Natural World.* Boston: Houghton Mifflin Harcourt, 2012.

INDEX

deodorant, 45
de-scenting, 45–46, 56
dewclaws, 128–29
diagonal walking, 129, 132
Dickinson, Emily, 73
"Discover the Forest" campaign, 12
distractions, 55
dog
    movement patterns of, 129
    tracks by, 127, 130–31
down, 32
Drake, Tim, 59–60
drought, 117–18
Dunne, Pete, 153

E

eastern coyotes, 149, 164, 166
ecotone, 40, 42
edge area, 40, 42
egg laying, 133
Einstein, Albert, 126
elimination behaviors, 86, 134
emotional energy, 178
empathy, 76
endosymbiosis, 96
energy conservation, law/rule of, 38,
    75–77, 87
environment(s)
    baseline and, 40
    as vulnerabilities, 117–20
environmental factors
    drought, 117–18
    flooding, 118–19
    temperature extremes, 119–120
    weather extremes, 119–120
    wildfires, 119
Erickson, Dan, 55
escape routes, 134
ethics, 24–27
ethogram
    description of, 80–81
    life cycle behaviors in, 81–91
    reproductive behaviors in, 91–94
    social behaviors in, 94–102
exoskeleton, 89, 114
extinction, 25, 189
"extreme drought," 118

extreme environments, three hours in, 28

F

fawns, 147
feelings, 176
*Field Guide to Tracking Mammals in the
    Northeast, A,* 125
*Field Guide to Venomous Animals and
    Poisonous Plants, A,* 20
field guides, 33, 42
field marks, 127–28, 132–36
"fight or flight" behavior, 76
fire, 29. *See also* wildfires
first aid, 29
fish, 107–08
fisher, 49, 69, 118, 123–24, 130–31, 150–51
fishing, 26
fleeing, 75
flooding, 19, 118–19
food
    for animals, 77, 79–80, 151
    extra, 30
    three weeks without, 28
footprints, 127–29
footwear, 32, 57
Foster, Steven, 20
fox walking, 46–47, 50–53, 61
foxes, 53, 73–74, 97, 148, 154, 159–60
freeze, 75, 77
frogs, 39–40, 65

G

gait, 129, 132
galloping, 132
garter snakes, 39, 81, 90, 111, 114, 151–53,
    167, 177–78
geese, 90, 100, 110
Glidden, Lily, 180
global climate change, 110–11
gloves, 32
Goodall, Jane, 80, 182
gray fox, 56, 72–74, 159
gray squirrels, 10, 65
great blue herons, 34, 36, 60, 69
great horned owls, 60, 69
grief, 101

ABOUT THE AUTHOR

Dave Hall is the founder of Primitive Pursuits, a youth-based nature awareness program offered in partnership with Cornell Cooperative Extension 4H of Tompkins County. A graduate of the State University of New York at Geneseo, he has worked as a naturalist and guide in Massachusetts, New Jersey, and New York and has taught for the Adirondack Mountain Club, the State University of New York at Cortland, Cornell Outdoor Education, and Ithaca College. Dave has studied wilderness survival at Tom Brown Jr.'s Tracker School and Ricardo Sierra's Earth Mentoring Institute, and with naturalist Jon Young.

With more than thirty years of experience in the field, he is an authority on the topic of primitive survival and nature awareness. His first book, *Winter in the Wilderness: A Field Guide to Primitive Survival Skills* (co-authored with Jon Ulrich), was a best seller for Cornell University Press and was awarded an Honorable Mention in the National Outdoor Book Awards.

MOUNTAINEERS BOOKS, including its two imprints, Skipstone and Braided River, is a leading publisher of quality outdoor recreation, sustainability, and conservation titles. As a 501(c)(3) nonprofit, we are committed to supporting the environmental and educational goals of our organization by providing expert information on human-powered adventure, sustainable practices at home and on the trail, and preservation of wilderness.

Our publications are made possible through the generosity of donors, and through sales of 700 titles on outdoor recreation, sustainable lifestyle, and conservation. To donate, purchase books, or learn more, visit us online:

MOUNTAINEERS BOOKS
1001 SW Klickitat Way, Suite 201 • Seattle, WA 98134
800-553-4453 • mbooks@mountaineersbooks.org •
www.mountaineersbooks.org

An independent nonprofit publisher since 1960

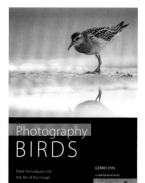
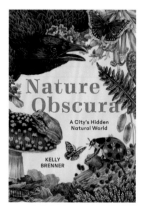